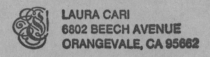

W9-BSL-995

LAURA CARI
6802 BEECH AVENUE
ORANGEVALE, CA 95662

Mourning Song

Mourning Song

⇶⇶⇶⇶⇶⇶⇶⇶⇶⇶⇶ ⇷⇷⇷⇷⇷⇷⇷⇷⇷⇷⇷

Joyce Landorf

FLEMING H. REVELL COMPANY

Old Tappan, New Jersey

Unless otherwise identified, Scripture references in this volume are from The Living Bible. Copyright 1971 by Tyndale House Publishers, Wheaton, Illinois 60187. All rights reserved.

Scripture references identified KJV are from the King James Version of the Bible.

Scripture references identified RSV are from the Revised Standard Version of the Bible. Copyrighted 1946 and 1952.

Excerpts from ON DEATH AND DYING by Elisabeth Kübler-Ross (Copyright © 1969 by Elisabeth Kübler-Ross) are used by permission of the publishers, Macmillan Publishing Co., Inc., New York.

Scripture quotations identified MLB are from MODERN LANGUAGE NEW TESTAMENT—THE NEW BERKELEY VERSION IN MODERN ENGLISH Copyright © 1945, '59, '69 by Zondervan Publishing House and are used by permission.

"A Psalm on the Death of an 18-Year-Old Son" is from *Psalms of My Life* by Joseph Bayly, Tyndale House Publishers, Wheaton, Illinois. Used by permission.

"The Sound of Music" is from THE SOUND OF MUSIC © Copyright 1959 by Richard Rodgers and Oscar Hammerstein II. Williamson Music, Inc., New York, N.Y., owner of publicational and allied rights for all countries of the Western Hemisphere. All Rights Reserved. Used by permission.

"The Grandfather" by Robert M. Howell is reprinted from THE CHRISTIAN by permission of The Christian Board of Publication, St. Louis.

Excerpts from THE RICHEST LADY IN TOWN by Joyce Landorf, Copyright © 1973 by the Zondervan Corporation are used by permission.

Poems "Teach Me to Walk Alone," "The Heart Held High," "Broken Dreams," "Remembered Dreams," "Friends," and "The Other Side," by Martha Snell Nicolson are from *Her Best for the Master* copyright 1964, Moody Press, Moody Bible Institute of Chicago. Used by permission.

"The False Friends" is from THE PORTABLE DOROTHY PARKER. Copyright 1926, 1954 by Dorothy Parker. Reprinted by permission of The Viking Press, Inc.

"Go Down Death—A Funeral Sermon" is from GOD'S TROMBONES by James Weldon Johnson. Copyright 1927 by The Viking Press, Inc., Copyright © renewed 1955 by Grace Nail Johnson. Reprinted by permission of The Viking Press, Inc.

Library of Congress Cataloging in Publication Data

Landorf, Joyce.
    Mourning song.

    1. Death. I. Title.
BT825.L35   248'.86   74-9938
ISBN 0-8007-0680-3

Copyright © 1974 by Fleming H. Revell Company
All Rights Reserved
Printed in the United States of America

This book is lovingly dedicated to

Von Letherer

A man who has courageously faced and coped with death and dying for all of his thirty-seven years.

His life as a dauntless Christian and his remarkable silence through the years of his pain-filled illness have honed and refined him into a dangerously beautiful, Christlike man.

The song of mourning constantly swirls about him, yet the clear, ringing, dolce melody of Christ's love is never lost or obscured.

In hearing the spirited bravura of this man's music, our hearts have been lifted toward Christ and we have been deeply touched—we will never be the same again!

My thanks to

Brenda Arnold

For the song you lovingly played on your
typewriter—including both the rough draft
and the final manuscript of this book—
I thank you! Such talent!

Love,

JOYCE LANDORF

Contents

Mourning Song

1

The Appointment

And as it is appointed unto men once
to die . . .

HEBREWS 9:27 KJV

Several events in the 1960s severely rattled the cages of my mind.
I have never been the same since. A Pandora's box of painful experiences, unexplainable emotions, and hidden fears opened before me.

Like so many people, I simply did not anticipate these events happening to me. I know it is "appointed unto men once to die" and
while I had given my own dying a small amount of thought, I did
not think it too relevant to think or ponder about death or dying to
any large degree.

I was like an army general I met while I was singing and speaking
at a military base. We were having dinner and discussing some
important issues of life when he said something about letting his
wife handle all religious or spiritual areas of their life for both of
them.

"What would happen, General," I asked, "if for some reason you had a heart attack tonight and when you asked your doctor to level about it he told you that you would not live the day out? Would you be content to let your wife handle all spiritual subjects or would you take matters into your own hands and go directly to God?"

He put both elbows on the table, rested his chin in his hands, and looked at me for a long time. Finally he said, "Honey—I've just never given any thought to death, especially my own, and frankly, no one has ever asked me such a question."

I thought, "I can see how that's entirely possible." Our built-in death denial comes as easily as breathing. "Why be worried?" we think. "Why not just take death and dying when and where it comes? Why make out a will? Why talk of our wishes concerning a funeral? Why talk of death—ours *or* someone else's—when it's so depressing?"

Why indeed? Part of the answer lies in the unnerving fact that no matter how well prepared we are to face death and dying, it always catches us at the worst possible moment. It is always brutal except when we are willing to learn from the dying. Then it is just a little less brutal and for some reason we are able to endure with *some* fortitude.

Even now I would like to put off writing this book. Yet the final results in my life produced by these events have brought a large measure of meaning to the quality of my daily living. I must ignore their voices no longer even though these events concern one of the most powerful fears of our life—death and dying.

The first of the events happened early in the sixties. Our son Rick was twelve years old; our daughter Laurie, just ten. To our great surprise I became pregnant, and after the most difficult pregnancy I'd ever experienced, I gave birth to a baby boy.

My husband Dick and I named him David—after the sweet, gifted singer of the Psalms.

His eyes were angelic sky blue and his head was covered with fine, corn-silk-golden hair. It was *instantaneous* love just to look at him.

We never found out if he would sing as his famous namesake had because David took one look around, thought about it for one long day, and went straight back to God without a backward glance.

Months later I was still wandering in the wilderness of grief, utterly devastated. I tried to find my way out—without letting too many people know I was lost—but the map books I read were filled with sticky-sweet poems and unreal directions.

One year after David's funeral my aunt called me. She said our darling Grandpa Uzon had felt chest pains that morning. He had awakened her and then calmly returned to his living room to wait for the doctor and fireman rescue team.

By the time help arrived, Grandpa had caught his flight home and was winging his way upward.

When no one close to you has ever died, and then when two loved ones are taken in one year, you feel just like Humpty Dumpty. You've fallen off the wall and you know all the king's horses and all the king's men are never going to be able to put you together again.

Having two die in one year did not in any way prepare me for a third death, either.

Nine months after I sang for Grandpa's funeral, I had to surrender another, my fifty-seven-year-old mother, to the waiting arms of God.

I remember I was utterly exhausted with waiting and watching around the clock for seven weeks at UCLA Medical Center. My husband asked me to come home, sleep in my own bed, and get some badly needed rest. I was in bed no more than a few hours when death played the meanest trick of all—it took her and I didn't even get to see her go!

The next months were the most puzzling times of my life. I had marvelous, incredible moments with God. His ability and power to comfort me were miraculous. But these moments were followed by weeks where I felt absolutely alone. Someone waved a magic wand and God simply did a disappearing act. My grief, my loneliness, sometimes my anger welled up over the top of me and no matter how hard I yelled, God did not seem to hear me.

Not long ago a woman recognized me in a TV studio and said she'd read my books and asked if I was writing another. When I told her yes and said that it was on death she replied, "Oh, I lost my teen-age daughter a few years ago." I asked her if she would share her reactions with me. She assured me she didn't mind talking about it at all. So she related the doctors' diagnosis of cancer in her daughter, months of illness, and finally, the girl's death.

I asked, "Tell me—how did you cope with your grief after she died?"

"Oh, my dear," she said, looking directly at me, "I didn't *have* any grief—none at all. God took it *all* away from me."

Now, I love God with all my heart—this woman did too—what had she done that I had failed to do? I rephrased my question: "Go back to when you were told by the doctors that your daughter had cancer—before she died—how did you handle the grief of *that* news?"

She stared at me for a second or two and said, "I already told you. God took away my grief—I did not have grief—in fact, I didn't even shed a tear."

Long after the lady left I stood there remembering the many months of grief, tears, anger, and fragmentation I'd lived through after the deaths of my baby, my grandfather, and my mother.

I remembered that I thought I'd never be able to understand anything about death and dying. Then God used (of all things!) *Life* magazine. Just before the sixties came to an end, an exciting article appeared in *Life*. It was by the brilliant and sensitive Dr. Elisabeth Kübler-Ross, and in this short but moving article she answered many of my questions on death and dying.

Doctor Ross wrote of the five emotional stages a terminal patient experiences once he knows he is going to die. The first denial, then anger, bargaining, depression, and finally, acceptance. She gained her knowledge by talking with over two hundred terminally ill patients and her work is compiled in her book *On Death and Dying*.

I was stunned by the article because I'd watched all of those stages in my mother, but I was even more fascinated by the fact that in *my* bereavement I had identified with each and every stage and so did all the members of my family.

We had gone through denial, anger, bargaining, and depression into acceptance and then back again to *repeat* some stages. Later as I read her whole book it stirred my soul toward facing the realities of not only the dying of others, but my own death as well.

Reading it also marked the beginning of my most spiritually soul-searching times before God. I went back to God's Word—the Bible

—and began to see clearly answers that had been invisible before.

This period in my life marked, too, the first time in two years that I was able to find workable solutions to slowing down the flow of my hemorrhaging grief.

I am not writing about these experiences out of a medically or scientifically acquired knowledge—although I have read extensively and talked with some of the finest professionals in medicine today. I am not a doctor.

Neither am I writing about coping with death and dying from a theological position—although I believe Jesus Christ is the Son of God, the very One who died using His own life and body as a sacrifice for my sins. I have asked Him into my life and I am joyous at being known as a *Christian*. I am not a minister.

I am not writing out of a professionally educated knowledge either—although I work with one of America's most gifted psychologists, Dr. James Dobson. I am not a psychologist, counselor, or social worker.

I am putting these thoughts down from the feeling level of my heart.

A friend once said, "If there is to be an honest approach to death it must be with childlike feeling. It must be couched and surrounded by trust, honesty, and openness."

It is the feeling level of our souls that death chooses to make its central target. Feeling is where death sights, aims, and scores its most accurate bull's-eye. No one, experiencing death or sitting by the dying, has ever escaped its penetrating message.

I'll admit I didn't enjoy learning the messages about death. I don't like growing pains any more now than I did when my bones ached with growth during my adolescent development. However, if we ever stop learning and become know-it-alls we really stop being alive to life.

I am not writing this book to a select few. It would be unrealistic to write it only to bereaved parents, a grieving child, a shattered teen-ager, or for a floundering widow. Death is a very real part of living and comes to *every* person as surely as they are born. Death comes to all of us.

Putting our head ostrich-style in the sand of ignorance, hoping death will be postponed or go away altogether, is wasted insanity.

Ignoring the subject can only harm us immeasurably when death's icy hand reaches out and grips us or one of our loved ones. The unshatterable fact is that, whether we like it or not, we all keep our appointment with death. Since it happens to all of us then the big question is not, "Will I die?" but, "How shall I *live* until I *die?*"

The great theologian, Paul Tillich, questioned:

If one is not able to die, is he really able to live?

It is my hope that this book will help you to be willing to accept the realities of facing death, and that, there in your newfound willingness, God will begin to shed a new light on your abilities to live —really live.

People who are willing to take up the enormous task of communicating their fears or feelings, who discuss—even reluctantly—their wishes about death and dying, and those who make the effort to allow God to work *through* their grief *with* them, seem to be best equipped to live life to its fullest. Life, as Jesus intended, was meant to be lived abundantly. It was not to fill a cup halfway, but to go *past* the brim and overflow.

Those who live the abundant life seem to seize each experience, tragic or joyous, and squeeze every drop of learning out of it into their cup of life. Some of us are envious of the high-graded quality of their life-style. But we have forgotten what price that kind of honesty and courage has cost.

Someone once wrote, "Some die without having really lived, while others continue to live in spite of the fact that they have died."

David, the Psalmist, really experienced living life because he was well acquainted with grief, sorrow, and loss. He worked through these times of bereavement and penned these remarkable words on the type of life-style he desired.

Lord, help me to realize how brief my time on earth will be. Help me to know that I am here for but a moment more. We glide along the tides of time as swiftly as a racing river, and vanish as quickly as a dream. We are like grass that is green in the morning but mowed down and withered before the evening shadows fall. Seventy years are given us! And some may even live to eighty. But even the best of these years are often emptiness and pain; soon they disappear, and we are gone. Teach us to number our days and recognize how few they are; help us to spend them as we should.

Psalms 39:4; 90:5, 6, 10, 12

This book, then, is not really about death, but rather about life. It's about handling and coping with our living after a loved one has gone and of numbering and spending our own days more carefully while we are here.

If we live this way then when death does appear we will not spin a dark, opaque cocoon around our life and miss its meaningful stages or fear its shocking emotions.

We will know and recognize death. We will feel the pain of loss when our loved ones are gone. But we need not stand and try to work through our widely changing emotions and feelings alone. We can trust in God's restorative powers.

Then when death comes not to a loved one, but to us, we can hold our heads high. We can understand—at least in part—that what is most important is not *how* or *where* we die, but *what we did with life* while we were here and able.

Oh, dear Lord, this book is painful to write because of all the remembering I must do. But I want to write with an acutely sensitive pen—so don't spare memories for me.

I know *now* (hindsight is great) that You directed my way through my losses, but forgive me for thinking You had abandoned me. You were there, walking with me, in the valley of the shadow of death, but my tears blinded me. I marvel at Your endless patience with me, Lord. Had I been You, I would have given up.

Thank You for leading me to the right books—both on the newsstand and in the Bible. What You taught me through them has increased the capacity and quality of my very existence. I'm glad—no, honored—that the way was so hard. It was the vehicle for You to use in my life in a meaningful, mighty way.

Remember, Lord, just a few weeks before she died, my mother pointed her finger at me and said these words: "Honey, for thirty-four years I've taught you how a Christian should live. Now I'm going to show you how one dies." Remember?

Well, Lord, take those priceless lessons and mold them into this book.

Sometime, when I am to keep my appointment with death, I want to have learned those lessons and lived so full a life for You that I am able to say with David the Psalmist:

But as for me, my contentment is not in wealth but in seeing you and knowing all is well between us. And when I awake in heaven, I will be fully satisfied, for I will see you face to face.

                                                                Psalms 17:15

So, dear Saviour,

> If I should die
> Before I wake,
> I pray thee, Lord,
> My soul to take.
>
> And as for those I love and leave behind
> Let them remember my last plea—
> I've gone home to God—I *am not dead*
> So let them sing no sad mourning songs for me.

2

Scared to Death of Dying

The fear of death is worse than death.
ROBERT BURTON

After she had transacted my banking business, the teller looked
across her counter at me and said, "Okay, Joyce, tell me what you
are writing now!"

"Well," I began, "actually I'm in between books at the moment,
finishing one and about to start another."

"The one you're going to start—what's it about?" she asked.

"It's a book on death," I started to explain, but she broke in and
said, "That one—write it for me!"

"Why?" I asked.

"Oh, because I'm scared to death of dying." Her statement wasn't
meant to be a play on words and she was quite serious.

"Do you mean you are afraid of the actual process of dying and
how it will feel?" I questioned.

She thought for a second or two and then said, "No, I guess I'm not so afraid of dying myself, but I have this terrible fear about the possibility of my husband dying. What would I do? How would I survive? The whole thing really scares me."

Her "terrible fear" is familiar to all of us although the fear of death strikes in different ways with different individuals.

A child comes home from school, finds his mother, brothers, and sisters gone and is gripped by the fear they have left him or worse— they have died.

The bride begins to suffer from the same fear when her young husband has not returned home at the accustomed, usual time.

The man driving along the freeway sees an accident ahead of him involving a car exactly like the one his wife drives and fear covers him with a wave of nausea and perspiration.

The parents grip each other's hands as the doctor says, "I'm sorry, but the tests show your son has . . . ." Fear plugs up their hearing and they miss the diagnosis.

The teen-ager goes to the mortuary to pay his respects to a friend, but he leaves instantly and splatters his fear on the sidewalk outside.

The grandmother hides her fears about her husband dying during the day, but each night dreams he *has* died and in her dream she endlessly drowns in a sea of fearful loneliness.

A man actually in the process of dying shares his greatest fear with his son when he says, "Teddy, boy—when I die, make sure I'm really dead before they put me into the ground. When I was little I was accidentally locked into a closet and the fear of being buried alive started there—so make sure I'm dead."

The young boy experiences the agony of his greatest fear as he feels that dying will mean facing the end of existence as he knows it with no experience to guide him into the unknown.

A doctor, in order to disguise his own fears about death, blurts out gruffly to a woman, "Your husband is dead," and abruptly turns on his heel and leaves her in her shock.

Another doctor, because he feels a patient's death means *he* has failed, makes it a policy to never quite level with a patient. He denies death and its finality another way by rarely, if ever, attending a funeral.

This "terrible fear" catches all of us. No matter how we look at it, even as mature, steady, reliable Christians, death is a very scary thing—if not scary, at least extremely distateful. Our fear of it has always risen to the top of our minds and probably always will.

There is another aspect of our fear and it concerns not death, but the actual method of our dying.

We wish death (*if* it should ever come to us) would arrive when we are eighty-five years of age—after a nice, full life. We all want death to come peacefully and preferably in our sleep. In the back of our minds lurks the dark thought that death, when it comes to us, may be violent or without dignity.

We are not willing to face the fact that death may come in a totally different way than we thought.

In our minds we conjure up the peaceful deathbed scene. At the moment of death the aged loved one sits up or opens his eyes and then gives some beautiful last words involving spiritual insights or some descriptions of his first glimpses into heaven. When this happens we breathe a sigh of farewell and write about the beauty of it all. But what of the times when death comes and all dignity vanishes? We are reluctant to even think it may happen in this way.

When I asked the nurse how my mother died, she answered with a considerable amount of relief in her voice, "Oh, very quietly in her sleep." I've always wondered if that was true or was the nurse shielding me and just being kind by not telling me *exactly* how my mother died.

Knowing my outspoken mother, I tend to think she probably, just before her last breath, said, "Oh, come on Lord, for goodness sake, hurry it up!"

Joe Bayly, in telling of his five-year-old son's death by leukemia, relates that his son died a violent death while hemorrhaging and screaming for a bedpan. For two years Joe could not speak of the manner of his son's death.

A chaplain I know once told me that since he had been torpedoed and rescued at sea and had escaped death on several other occasions, he was not afraid to die. However, he said he was concerned about whether or not he would die "like a man."

As I have already said, we want death to come to us when we are in our eighties, with dignity and during our sleep. I suspect my

aunt is still trying to put the memory of my grandmother's recent
death to rest in her mind. It was in such dreadful contrast to my
grandfather's quiet homegoing. My grandmother, in her eighties, a
strong, marvelous Christian, died with no last words of comfort or
wisdom—and she did not die peacefully, or with dignity, although
her soul belonged to God. She died being held upright on the toilet
just as her bowels completely broke and gushed from her. My aunt,
holding her, had no way of retaining the contents of her own churn-
ing stomach. So my grandmother died with the unbelievable stench
of her broken bowels swirling below and covered above with my
aunt's irrestrainable vomit. It was a moment of horror. I doubt that
my aunt will ever be able to relate Grandma's death to the poetically
beautiful verse in the Bible about how precious, to God, is the death
of a saint. My grandmother, delightful child of God, and, yes, saint—
did not die in an ideally serene atmosphere and it was anything but
a precious homegoing. It was a totally unforeseen nightmare.

So we fear the method of dying as well as death itself. If it is
not a conscious fear, it may well be an unconscious concern.

Since death only happens once to us, we are at as much of a loss
to explain it as we are to explain our own birth.

We cannot remember our time before birth in our mother's womb,
nor can we remember anything about the process of being born. We
simply did it. But the process of dying does worry us. How will we
react? How will it be? When will it happen? One smart aleck I
know and love said, "Oh, Joyce, don't worry about dying—you'll
make it! Everyone does, you know." (Thanks, friend, I needed
that!)

I suppose what we really fear about death the most is all the
unanswered questions and the myriad pile of "unknowns."

Most of us are not as open, honest, or outspoken about our fears
as the teller in my bank. However, death still is a top-priority fear.
The French philosopher, Pascal, noted that high priority when he
remarked, "We spend our lives trying to take our minds off death."

I have been to a thousand funerals either as a mourner, soloist, or
both, but believing that someday my husband or children will lie
in a box, surrounded by satin and flowers, is simply too incredible
to seriously understand. My fear surges up and around me with such

intensity I force myself to mentally escape into pleasant, wonderful memories to obliterate it.

How is it, as a Christian, the fear of death can do this to me? I have reasoned with myself over this question and I have thought, "I am confident about my position as a child of God. I have been a Christian for many years now and know full well where a Christian goes when he or she dies, yet why does death (at least initially) terrify me?" I *know* intellectually in my mind and emotionally in my heart that my Saviour and Lord has removed death's sting—I know that as a Christian I have the *only* hope in death—so why does this fear persist? Why is it each and every time I enter a hospital, for any reason, I feel the fearful sting of death? The aroma of antiseptic solutions, the noise of clattering trays, and the attendants hurriedly rushing by, pushing gurneys or carts, make me want to run out of there as fast as a scared jackrabbit in the middle of a traffic-jammed freeway.

"Men fear death because they refuse to understand it," said Cyrus L. Sulzberger in his book *My Brother Death*.

So here's when we begin—with our fears. It starts with trying to understand this mysterious process and trying with all our minds and souls to prepare ourselves for death's inevitable tap on the heartbeat of our existence.

During my process of trying to understand my fears an incident happened in the foothills above our city. It shaved off a fair amount of fear from my soul. I am indebted to my pastor, Dr. Ted Cole, for leading my mind through the maze of this lesson.

A young boy was bitten by a rattlesnake while he was hiking up one of our foothill canyons with his dad. The boy's father rushed him to the nearest hospital and after many hours of working on him, doctors finally saved his life. It had been a very close call and at times the doctors had lost hope, but he did pull through. Our newspaper ran the story and printed a picture of the smiling little boy sitting up in bed with his relieved parents standing by.

Our pastor brought the story to his pulpit the next Sunday and enlightened our hearts toward understanding our fears of death.

He read the article and then where the story ended he went on and asked us to pretend with him. We were to pretend that after the boy's life was saved somebody went back to the canyon, located the ledge where the boy had been climbing, and found the very same rattlesnake that had bitten him. Then, after catching the rattlesnake they took it to a veterinarian and had the snake's venom completely removed, making the snake absolutely nonpoisonous. Then a doctor or someone took the now nonpoisonous snake into the boy's room. It was shown to the boy and someone explained that it was harmless now and no longer deadly. Then the boy was asked if he wanted to hold the snake and keep it as a pet.

At this point Dr. Cole questioned his congregation: "Do you think any amount of reasoning or explaining could get the boy to reach out and touch that snake—much less keep it?"

The answer was obviously a resounding no! The boy would still be scared to death of that snake. There is no way he would be willing to accept this particular snake because to him it still would look deadly and wouldn't look one bit changed. No one would be able to convince the boy that it was all right. The hospital would have echoed his terrified screams.

Here, then, is part of the answer as to why death frightens us so much. While, as a Christian, I *know* Christ has removed the sting of death and death can never kill me for eternity—*death still exists*. It is still fearfully ugly and repulsive. I probably will never be able to regard, imagine, or fantasize death as being a loving friend.

Whenever and wherever death and dying connects with us—no matter how strong we are in our Christianity or how well we are prepared for it—it still slides and slithers into our lives and freezes us with fear. Such is the nature of death.

With a touch of fear in her voice, my mother some years ago, while she was in her late forties, talked briefly about her own dying. I was over at her house helping her to clean out a long-neglected linen closet. She'd been a little less noisy than usual so I said, "Penny for your thoughts, Mother." She looked down, straightened some bath towels, and without looking up said, "Well, I'm not trying to be morbid, but lately I've had this feeling that I'll not live too many years longer. I feel I'll never see Marilyn or Cliff grown or married. In fact, I don't think God is going to give me the normal seventy-five-year life-span."

A small chill ran down my back. She had voiced what most of us think (once in a while) about our own dying. Sometimes during a blue mood we have all fantasized about how it would be to die young or suddenly or right now, and we spend a brief time on the "what ifs" of our dying. I was tempted to brush Mother's remark away, pat her on her head, and say something smart like, "Honey, you're too mean to die." But the fear that it might be true hovered in the hallway like a faded fragrance from an old spice bouquet hidden among the linens and I couldn't be smart *or* funny about it.

The phone rang and easily stopped our conversation and then time diverted it into a new direction. Neither of us brought it up again. Since then I've wondered about that day and have pondered if the phone had not rung when it did if she would have gone on and told me her "big secret," the secret which lent authenticity to her feelings of dying. I'll never know.

She alone had access to some information and she kept it from us. Years before our day by the linen closet she had discovered small lumps on her left breast. Her fears about the unpronounceable word *cancer* made her lock her secret up and she deliberately threw away the key. She was like others of her generation. If they even suspected cancer, they would quietly sentence themselves to death. They would seek no medical help. They were sure all the doctors wanted to do was "cut into them." Tragically, they would hurry death along for sure. They told no one because "after all, it was probably already too late" or so they rationalized. Many of this generation would die *needlessly* because they had not sought help early enough and many, like my mother, would die saying, "Joyce, don't you *dare* do what I did. You promise me you'll go to your doctor for regular checkups."

There was another reason for locking up her secret and it had to do with her strong faith in God.

She was on completely familiar terms with Almighty God. She had watched Him, all through her life, directing her paths. He had rescued, healed, and comforted her each year of her life she had served Him. "He'll take care of those lumps," was her reasoning. So, in childlike faith, she gave Him her dreadful secret and left it with Him. It was God's problem, not hers, and God would handle it. I'm sure she never intended for any of us to ever know so she never told us about the lumps, only about the feeling she'd die early.

Some might say we found out later accidentally, but I think not. God surprised us by giving her secret away for her.

It was a few short years after we'd cleaned out the linen closet when one day she turned the corner in the hall, misjudged the position of the kitchen doorway, and ran smack into it. Later that night she was undressing just as my father came into the bedroom. It took no more than a second's glance at the ugly bruise and swelling on Mother's breast before he told her he was taking her to the doctor the first thing in the morning. Her secret was out so she meekly agreed to see their doctor.

The next day, my father phoned me and told me of Mother's bruise and her trip to the doctor. It had taken a short time to discover larger groupings of lumps, but it took no time at all to put her into the hospital and schedule surgery for the next day.

As I drove to the hospital the next afternoon, I remembered my conversation about her not living a full life. She was now fifty-four years old. Words like *tumor, cancer,* and *biopsy* all floated in and out of my mind that day. I began the very first serious thinking about her death. It seemed to me that death never really hits us all at once, but rather in surges like the waves of the sea. Some waves cause little more than ripples and then the sea becomes still—others begin building and one by one they get larger. Soon the seventh wave builds up its enormous strength and energetically hits the beach with unleashed force.

Daily we lose a little more ground. Our old tissue dies and drops and the new develops—only to complete the circle and die. Paul, in the New Testament, said we die daily. "How true," I thought as I drove.

When I reached Mother's room she was sleeping lightly. I touched her face and she opened her eyes, recognized me, started to smile, and then remembered something disturbing. She said, "Oh, Joyce, they took it. It's gone. I have no . . . ." She couldn't say the word *breast*.

Even though my generation is far more well-read and open than hers about the care and treatment of breast cancer, I still remember the words *radical mastectomy* clobbering the breath right out of my lungs. The small box of fear inside me was rapidly expanding and I took on a whole shipment of anxiety.

Mother was explaining to me what had transpired and her tone of voice was the most bewildering I'd ever heard.

"When I came in yesterday, I signed some papers—I didn't read too much of them because the words were very medical-sounding. I didn't know I was giving them permission to take my . . . I was drowsy with some shot—I didn't know—Joyce, they amputated *me* —they took *me*—it's gone," she finished, shaking her head in disbelief.

"Mother, why didn't you tell anyone about the lumps when you first found them? Why didn't I know?" I whispered.

"Oh, honey, I just thought—oh, you know—the Lord has always taken care of every need—I didn't want to bother you about it," she explained.

I left her bed later and went out to find her doctor. He saw me coming down the hall, stuck out his hand, grabbed mine, and said, "I'm pretty sure we got it all." Those words washed another surge of fear over my soul. I managed to form the question, "Malignant?"

"Yes," he answered.

A friend of mine wrote, "Normally we think of fear as a negative force in our lives; however, it can and does perform at least one positive function for us—it wakes us up! Not many people fall asleep when the adrenaline is flowing."

That day well marked the beginning of the big adrenaline flow in my life and after that falling asleep became a difficult task.

However, that big, new, ugly fear caused me to look long and seriously at my mother. I was filled with a desire to know all about her in every way and dimension. I also took a good, long look at my own feelings and fears about death and my (sometime in the future) death. I noticed that while the fire of fear certainly still burned, it seemed to be contained and confined a bit.

I began to feel a compelling urgency about my life and the time allotted to me. What was I doing with my years? How was I spending my life's energies? What if I had ten days or thirty years to live? Was I eagerly participating in the celebration of life—or was I plodding dully along from one rut to another?

I decided I would really train myself to see all I could see, hear all I could hear, and be all I could be for however many years I had. It was, has been, and is an exhausting decision, but worth it.

I am grateful to God for the lessons the fear of death has taught me.

I hate the method God used—losing a child and grandfather and finally my mother—but experiencing those fears rearranged many of my life's priorities and goals.

I began to consider death and dying in very personal terms. I realized that my attitude, my ability to cope, and my acceptance of my own eventual death would depend heavily on how I had faced or avoided death in general.

I now know the fear of death is a *universal* human trait built into all of us. I must not be shocked or surprised by it in my own life. I must not be hard or judgmental toward others when I see it in theirs.

I must be willing to admit that dying is not always well preceded by advance notice, but that it can be sudden, violent, and with complete loss of dignity.

A seventeen-year-old boy like Mike can fall asleep at the wheel of his car, hit a tree, and be instantly incinerated to death. A girl like Debbie can be kidnapped, raped, and murdered within a span of five torturous hours. A grandmother like mine can die in undignified violence. Such is the method of death sometimes.

I must hold high in my heart the moving truth that all of these who died in sudden vulgarity have reached their ultimate destination of heaven. In spite of the transportation used and the unacceptable method of traveling, they have completed their trip and have arrived. They are now gloriously alive!

If I am willing to lay my fears out on the table and acknowledge their presence, I'm halfway home to mastering a degree of acceptance about them. I can even begin to see a little hope and healing taking place within me.

However, because the fear of death and dying is never fully conquerable in us, I am like the little boy, recovering from his snakebite. I am unable to pet the rattlesnake.

My mother was released from the hospital and came home in what can only be described as high, joyous spirits. It was as if she'd deliberately forgotten to pack her fears or her disappointments in her suitcase. She came home from the hospital without them. I was baffled by the change of emotions. She treated her surgery with the same importance one attaches to an uncomplicated tonsillectomy done in a doctor's office under a local anesthetic.

She was an avid reader and I wondered how in the world she'd missed all those magazine articles on cancer and particularly breast cancer. I had no way of knowing that because she knew she had lumps she'd studiously avoided reading anything with the word *cancer* in it.

The only plans she had were to recover. I was pleased about this mentally healthy attitude, but puzzled again because she would not let me mention anything about her surgery, her illness, or the word *cancer*. Once when I tried she quickly shushed me up with, "Now, now, the doctors got 'it' all." Then she followed that with, "And now I'm going to get well."

She had never been of the Christian Scientist denomination or persuasion, but at one point I told her she'd make a great one! She just laughed and told me (again) I was taking her surgery too seriously. God had taken care of her as He promised and now there was nothing more to worry about. "The battle's over and won!" she said victoriously.

I did not realize until many months later that she had gone into the closet of complete denial and had firmly shut the door behind her.

3

Oh, God—No!

You can't heal a wound by saying it's
not there!

JEREMIAH 6:14

A car carrying six teen-agers to a football game swerved at a high
rate of speed and crashed into a concrete wall. The driver of the
car, a sixteen-year-old girl, trapped inside, listened to the sounds
of dying coming from her five friends. One thing each of them said,
the lone survivor reported, was the phrase, "Oh, God—no."

Whether it is the knowledge of our own imminent death or the
news of someone else's, the reaction seems to be the same. It does
not matter if it is a sudden death like the teen-agers' in this tragic
accident or a death painfully fought against and drawn out for years
—the moment of death is always too much to understand. The knowledge of death brings an immediate crisis to our lives and our crisis
centers on denial. The word *denial* becomes the most difficult
word in our language to learn or even pronounce out loud.

The second we are notified of the presence of death we *cannot* believe it and all our emotions gather forces to shout, "No!"

An older woman, upon learning her husband of fifty-six years had died suddenly while she was outside gardening, looked incredulously at her granddaughter and said, "Oh, no—that's simply not true. Why, he wouldn't do that without me. We were supposed to go together."

It's simply too incredible to comprehend never seeing one *here* again. It's too unthinkable to imagine what the silence would be like to never hear one's voice again. It's totally unimaginable to fathom living each day without that one!

Upon learning about the death of a loved one our thoughts may be stunned, fuzzy, or blurred, but one thing we know for sure— *it is not true.* Oh, how we cling to the hope the news is not true.

When my husband leaned over my bed as I lay in the hospital and said, "Hon, it's all over. David is with the Lord," my first words were, "Oh, no."

Months before, my doctors had suggested I prepare myself because our baby, with the Rh-negative blood factor, might not survive birth. But even with all the preparation my heart let me do —I wonder if I would have *ever* been really ready for the blow. I doubt it.

If you told me this second that my husband or one of our children were suffering from a terminal illness or had just suddenly died— I would react with the same, "Oh, no." We have, for several years, talked freely about death and dying with our entire family. I suppose if any family has communicated, discussed, and faced death and dying, it's ours, but still the death knowledge—when it comes— is *impossibly* heavy. I know, even with preparation, *denial* would swell like an ugly bruise immediately after death's heavy blow. While we can prepare ourselves for death—up to a point—we rarely are able to adjust with calmness and instant acceptance when the moment comes.

A man relived his moments of denial when he heard the doctor diagnose his own about-to-be-fatal disease when he recalled, "The doctor's words hit me with the sting of dynamite." Later he described denial symptoms as burning sensations in his chest, poundings in his head, numbness in his arms and legs, and feet that had "gone all rubbery" under him. Instant denial hits not only verbally with, "Oh, no," but physically devastates us as well.

Not long ago I had a long interview with the brilliant and sensitive surgeon Dr. James White. Both Jim and his wife are dear friends to us and both possess absolutely marvelous Christian personalities. I wondered aloud with Jim about the whys of death denial and we talked of his terminally ill patients.

Since he understood full well the emotional problems and crises the death knowledge would produce in patients and their families, I asked, "Do you always come straight out and level with a patient and his family about death?"

His answer came slowly and thoughtfully: "About 99 percent of the time." Then he added, "But I definitely postpone the news if it in any way jeopardizes the patient's well-being." He did not tell patients of their true condition, for instance, who were in danger of cardiac arrest, when the news might bring on the fatal attack. Also, he did not tell a patient immediately out of surgery or even one day out of intensive care while the patient was still physically critical. However, if a patient right out of surgery did ask a direct question about death or dying, he said he would buy time (usually a day or two) by referring to "waiting for test results." He did this only in cases where he felt the knowledge of their exact condition would be extremely detrimental to their general health and well-being.

The 99 percenters were kindly and gently told the truth. My talk with Jim that night confirmed for me once again that I would want a doctor to treat me exactly as Jim treats his patients. I would want, if it were at all possible, to know the extent of damages and the professional opinion of my doctor—even if it meant his telling me of my death.

"Please promise me," I asked of my husband, "that you will do everything to level with me—it would be unfair to leave me out of such happenings. There might be things I'd want to do or say, and I'd be better equipped to leave you (and vice versa) if I knew of my own impending death."

I remember the family who did not know the father was dying of cancer until his last three months. He told them the nature of his illness at that point and then as his condition worsened they said their good-byes and talked freely of death and dying. They were all with him when he died. Later, when his will was read, the lawyer gave the widow and her children a box of recorded tapes. The father had taped them eight or nine months before he died, when he was still feeling fine, but just after his doctor had told him of his condition being terminal. For weeks he had recorded tapes to each member of his family. His children were given tapes and special words for each of their upcoming birthdays—through the teens and to their twenty-first year. His wife was left tapes to help her adjust to everything—from check writing to his wishes about her remarrying again. There were special messages for the family's first Christmas without him and even a tape for his first grandchild for whenever the child was born.

He was able to leave his family these treasured tapes because of a wise doctor who told him the nature of his illness and from his own acceptance. Recording those tapes was probably the hardest thing he ever decided to do—but he'd put down his denial and his wife and family were sustained for years by the legacy so lovingly left by this man.

In my own case, I'd want to be told—if it were at all possible.

Doctor White is one of those gifted men who can handle the telling of such news in the best possible way. I asked him if he had some kind of a formula for divulging this information, but what I particularly wanted to know was—if he had a whole roomful of young doctors, what would he tell them about breaking this kind of news.

He told me the main point of teaching young doctors about working with the dying would involve a procedure of four words: *gradual with the information.*

However, when death was not drawn out, but very sudden, the "gradual information" would be handled differently. Later I'll share his ways of informing loved ones of a patient's sudden death.

But for the slowly dying patient, a wise doctor will watch carefully the patient's responses and reactions and give information out as the patient is able to take it in. If the patient asks a direct question, the caring doctor will give a direct answer. Dr. White told me that it was very important for the doctor to not, at any time, lie to a patient. He said he did not lie, even by implication. He felt it was absolutely imperative to establish an honest level of communication between patient and doctor.

"Very often," he continued, "a patient will ask, 'Is it a tumor?' I'll answer, 'Yes.' Then a day, maybe two days later, the same patient will look up at me and ask, 'Malignant?' I'll say, 'Yes,' and depending on the patient's responses after that, I will talk with him as long, or as little, as he wants."

This wise doctor, in giving gradual yet honest information, is giving the patient's right to denial a chance to work itself out. His sensitivity to the patient's questions and his alertness to their specific needs make him a rare doctor.

The more we talked about his views on helping patients and families accept death, the more I became terribly aware of the Christlike, loving concern hovering over this man like a heavenly mantle. I do not mean to sound maudlin or overly sentimental about such a man, but he is *rare!* Truly rare.

For years doctors have been so bogged down by their own fears and hang-ups regarding death they have, traditionally, been of very little help to the dying or their families.

They have been more than willing to teach us the entire birth process with printed information, long talks, or even classes. Over twenty years ago I took six weeks of classes from our doctor when I was pregnant with our first child. I was so well prepared by my doctor for the birth of our first child that I even had a checklist of hospital routine in my hand when I entered the hospital's labor room. The nurse in charge came in, talked with me a few minutes while I was in labor, and asked me how many other children I had. When I told her I was having my first, she said, "Oh, then you have got to be a Dr. Cartwright patient—right?"

"Yes," I replied. "How did you know?"

"All his patients are so well prepared to give birth, they come in with very few questions, familiar with hospital procedure, and fully accepting the birth process."

I know of no classes set up in any hospitals or doctors' offices to help the dying or the families of the dying to cope with the death process. The need for such classes or instruction is shockingly enormous.

From all I have read and heard, there is a high percentage of doctors who themselves need real help in telling a patient of his terminal illness. Up until a few years ago there were no classes on death and dying offered to medical students who would be dealing with dying almost daily in their practice. Even now there are only a few classes and seminars available to help doctors' understanding of death and treating the terminally ill.

Once a patient is dead it seems the doctor's work is over. The idea that the bereaved family desperately needs his healing services does not occur to him or, if it does, he does not see it as his responsibility. If the doctors, nurses, or clergy do not give help to the dying and their families—who will?

Professional people in medicine and the clergy are dealing with birth and death all the time. To be so feeble in our attempts to educate and equip them for the titanic task of facing and accepting death says much about our society's frantic denial of death.

My friend Dr. White had no training in death seminars, but his own acceptance of death and a God-given honesty and gentleness has made him outstanding in professional medicine as he works with a highly disturbing problem.

Doctor White told me his final goal in the formula for helping a person through the death-knowledge crisis was to hold out a glimmer of hope to the patient. No matter how slight the hope, how farfetched or illusive, he felt it was absolutely necessary to talk of hope with the patient. Maintaining his honesty, he would give no false hopes, but he would find some ray of hope to leave with his patient.

Stewart Alsop, a man dying of leukemia, in his excellent book *Stay of Execution,* says, "A man who must die, will die more easily if he is left a little spark of hope that he may not die after all. My rule would be: Never tell a victim of terminal cancer the whole truth—tell him that he *may* die, even that he will *probably* die, but do not tell him that he *will* die."

Nobody, not even the most brilliant of our professional medical scientists, knows exactly *when* or in what *way* death will come. They can give educatedly wise medical guesses and judgments, but death has its own way of surprising us and doing the unexpected. "Some patients," Dr. White said, "give all the various signs and signals of not lasting the night, yet the next morning's dawn finds them having passed the death crisis and well established into recovery. Still other patients slip away right before our astonished eyes. We are stunned and can only say, 'How did it happen?'" Another doctor said unbelievingly, "I was standing right next to her and I never even saw it coming!"

Much is unexplainable about death—hence our fearful hang-ups and our death-denial procedures.

Some doctors have allowed their own fears of death to rob them of all sensitivity. They develop a steellike shield of brusqueness. They abruptly announce, "He's gone," or, "It's over," and instantly beat a retreat from the room to avoid any emotional outburst from the family. Exactly at the moment when a family has the most anxiety-filled questions that desperately need to be answered, the doctor leaves. The nurse who has been so attentive and active around the patient suddenly clams up and claims instant ignorance after the patient's death.

Still other doctors, in their own death denial, rationalize that most dying patients do not want the truth so they should not be given the knowledge of the seriousness of their illness. "No good will come from it," they say. Or, if a patient's family tells the doctor, "Don't tell Aunt Ida she's dying, she won't be able to take it," he helps their (and his own) denial by respecting their wishes. I feel this type of thinking and judgment will seriously jeopardize the family's chances of moving into acceptance of death later on.

Doctor Kübler-Ross feels the question should not be, "Should we tell?" but, rather, "How do I share this with my patient?"

Many ministers are guilty of death denial, though it's played out in a little different way from a doctor. The minister occupies himself with "being there," or he becomes a highly trained nurse's aide and gets right to his "busy work" of shaving the patient or straightening out the tray on the nightstand. If the patient or his family really get down to talking about death and dying, the minister runs a swift retreat by reading a well-quoted psalm or ends all discussion by saying, "Let's have a word of prayer." His denial of death robs the dying and the family of one dying of the best tools in coping with death: the time of discussing their fears and denial problems.

One minister I know I'll always be grateful to is one who had properly accepted death and dying. He was a fantastic saint of God

named the Reverend Warner. Since he was in his seventies, everyone—young and old—called him Pop Warner. The morning after
our son had died, Pop stole quietly into my room. He touched my
arm and I woke to see him standing over me. "I know about your
baby," he said, not wasting any time.

"I'm glad to see you, Pop. Please sit down," I urged.

"No, my dear," he answered, "if I sit down I'll stay too long and
it will tire you, so I'll stand. Now, tell me, how is this going for
you?" Then that dear man stood and listened as I poured out my
anguished heart. He did not offer any advice, lecture, or words,
although he was more than capable. He did not busy himself with
taking out the wilted flowers beside my bed. He simply listened. He
looked me directly in the eye and heard my heart as I told him how
badly it was going with me. When I'd finally said everything I so
desperately needed to say, he bent over my bed and prayed, "Oh,
Lord, You are here and You've heard all that Joyce said. Now, You
know the way to heal her heart. Heal her quickly, Lord, and bind
up her wounds—we need her." And then, knowing it was hard for
me to believe David was really dead, he gently helped me take my
first tottering steps toward acceptance by adding, "And, dear Lord,
take loving care of that precious baby for Joyce."

An hour or so after he'd gone, I saw the little book on my nightstand. He had left it without telling me it was there. Over and over
in the following days I was to read and reread those Bible verses
in the little book and the memory of Pop Warner and the precious
words helped ease me out of denial into acceptance.

I thank God for ministers like Pop who never once evaded or
ignored my need to talk about our son's death—who didn't pat me
on the back telling me, "Everything is going to be all right," but
patiently let me explain why I *thought* everything was all wrong.

I thank God for doctors like Dr. White who are honest yet sensitive to the needs of the dying—who take time to help heal the pain
of bereaved families who must go on living after the patient dies.

I thank God, too, for the new breed of doctors like Dr. Elisabeth
Kübler-Ross who has taken on the monumental task of breaking
down the walls of our last great taboo—the dying process. Finally,
we are seeing a few courageous men and women who are stepping
forth to say, "Hey—let's not run and hide from this, and let's not

morbidly take death to our arms as a lover, but let's learn what we can from the dying and from each other about the death crisis!"

I'm grateful to God for the growing number of medical professionals, clergy, social workers, and counselors who are willing to help separate facts from fantasy—who are also willing to work and help people articulate their feelings about death.

We all have the general, vague feeling we *will* die sometime, but we all deny it by saying *but not now!* Most experts feel if we have expressed our feelings and fears to someone we are much more adept at handling death when it does come our way. There seem to be fewer surprises and fewer problems if death has not been completely blocked out or shoved under the rug in our conversations.

A beautiful young woman sat in my living room for a number of hours and told me about her husband's death. Just a bare two weeks before they had been climbing up a small canyon to cut down their Christmas tree when her husband, John, experienced unreal chest pains. A little more than twenty-four hours later this young, vibrant, twenty-six-year-old man was dead.

As she sat on my couch, Stephanie shed some tears and choked back some others, but on the whole she was poised and more than willing to share her innermost heart. When I asked her how her acceptance of John's death became real to her, she answered that they had prepared themselves. Theirs was a marriage with all channels of communication at a wide-open-throttle position. Both loved each other and God. Both had discussed their thoughts, dreams, ideas, and wishes. Both had given their lives for as much time as they had to being *God's* people. They had talked of death as routinely as they had talked of every subject under the sun. When death came, it was not as devastating as it could have been. She knew John's wishes. At one point she dropped her God-given acceptance and went back to denial as she said, "I can't believe it's happened."

I thought as I watched her that day, shaking her head in disbelief for just a second, that I wished I could be with her two months later rather than now in these first two weeks.

If we are Christians we experience a remarkable thing. Very often from the moment of someone's death, like in Stephanie's experience, we are surrounded, cushioned, and protected by God's beautiful cocoon of peace. We make a hundred different difficult decisions and we feel buoyed and spiritually uplifted. We go to the funeral and hope, glorious hope, pervades our hearts and minds.

But about two months later—when Christian friends have gone back to their work and have stopped praying—our world falls apart.

A widow who "did so well" at the funeral can't figure out the checkbook's balance system two months later and the tears of frustration cover her papers.

A mother who held all the family together when their daughter died falls apart three months later as she passes her daughter's old room.

A man who shed no tears at his wife's funeral is driving to work, hears his wife's favorite song on his car radio, and he has to pull off the road because his sobbing is uncontrollable.

They all wonder why at the funeral they were so calm, and why now, so much later, they can't seem to pull anything together. They are actually falling apart and it doesn't make sense. "How could we go through a funeral with our head up in complete acceptance and two months later be back in denial again? God was so real, so present, so comforting at first—now He seems to be gone."

About then some wise-enough-to-know-better-but-doesn't Christian is shocked by a widow's actions and questions, "Why, my goodness, what's happened to Mrs. So-and-So? She took her husband's death in her stride at the funeral—now look at her. I wish she'd snap out of this and be her normal self again. Too bad, though, I thought she was such a strong Christian. What's happened to her faith?"

Often we mistake the numbing effects of shock for "stride." We think because the widow is taking the funeral in her stride she's fine. Shock is the body's physical denial and protection and God allows us to be gently covered by it at the moments surrounding death.

Actually, the widow is experiencing the normal workings and 'pattern of denial and acceptance. God beautifully shields her at first to get her through, and then as the realities of death settle in, so does her grief.

As I talked with Stephanie that day I plainly saw and heard all about the beautiful way God eases us through the initially hard, brutal part of death. But I knew her time of waking to the reality of John's death and living and existing in her world *without* John would hit her later.

It *would* hit and it would have little to do with whether she was failing the Lord with a lack of faith or guilty of not trusting enough.

It has now been almost two months since I saw Stephanie, but just this week a friend of hers asked me to remember her in prayer. When I asked why, her friend said, "It's really funny. You know she took John's death so well, but now—now it's really hit her and she's having a rough time."

I am confident that Stephanie will work through this in the upcoming months. She is young and very willing to let God work out her griefs in her life. I know He will, but it will not be done overnight. She will need the loving prayers of family and friends just as much *now*, if not more, than when John died.

It's hard to grasp and understand the workings of denial—either the immediate "Oh, no" or the long, after-death kind, but I think how we cope with denial may be predetermined in our childhood.

I remember my father telling me about his own father's death. He told me about it a few months after my mother had died and I wished I'd known it earlier. Perhaps I could have understood a good many things relating to denial.

My father was about eight years of age, at school, when his teacher told him his aunt had come to take him home. Without a word, his aunt met him in the hall and hurriedly hustled him outside.

On the way home he asked, "Why did I have to leave school, Auntie?" With no show of any emotion, either facial or verbal, she abruptly stated, "Your father is dead." No explanation, no kind words, no empathy or sympathy followed. They rode home in stony silence. As the weight of his aunt's words began to crush him, my dad's tears started pouring down his face.

His aunt, seeing his tears, instantly slapped his face and yelled, "Stop that crying right now! Don't you *dare* cry."

Those moments, so long past, were the moments when Dad had shut off his feelings and emotions and they would live with him all his life.

When I was growing up I could never understand why my crying always upset my dad so much. He was always saying, "Joyce, you flush easily—now dry up."

He made crying something only a weak person would indulge in. Not until he recalled his father's death and that dreadful scene with his aunt did I begin to see where his attitude toward tears and death denial had started.

Our talking about tears and denial, even though it came after my mother's death, answered a number of questions. Had I known of Dad's background, I could have used that knowledge to a good advantage.

I wish I'd read Dr. Kübler-Ross's book, particularly the chapter on denial, before my mother's illness. It would have helped me to understand more about her denial as well as the other denial games we all played.

I would have been better equipped to have developed a patient, understanding attitude with Mother. I would probably not have reacted in anger toward my father and sister when I tried to cope with their denial. I could have been worlds more sympathetic in respecting their wishes to deny Mother's illness and subsequent death. I certainly could have helped them move through denial more smoothly into at least a partial acceptance.

Is all denial bad? I certainly thought so. I was one for facing the truth, no matter how painful. Somewhere along the line, maybe after years of trying to hold back or stop my tears, I felt that denial was a weak or stupid trait. I wish I'd known it's a terribly normal emotion that desperately needs to be voiced.

We all have a caring responsibility to the dying and to the bereaved even when we ourselves are part of the grieving family. One of the regrets of my life is that during my mother's illness I was not sympathetic with my family as I should have been. I was quite unprepared to see any denial in a mother who always met each and every problem in life *head-on*. It didn't dawn on me that denial would hit her—come on strong—then fade—then attack again. It simply never occurred to me that my father's bizarre actions, like buying my mother a four-hundred-dollar refrigerator just weeks before she died, were his patterns of denial. I had much to learn.

Had I known what I now know about denial, I could have coped with a different and larger capacity.

For instance, one year after her surgery my mother experienced every evidence of complete denial and without words friction ran high between us.

We never discussed the possibilities of other tumors or the need for a second mastectomy. She began cobalt treatments and still we did not talk about the dark shadows we both saw. We certainly never said the word *cancer*. Mother was only able to say *cancer* if she was talking about someone else's cancer. To my sister she called it "this sickness." I grew quite impatient with her.

When Christmas rolled around I was eager to set her straight about her blatant denial. I felt she should face up to the fact that she was showing evidences of advanced breast cancer. In a great burst of sincere stupidity, I wrote on the back of my Christmas card to her:

Dearest Mother,
  Knowing full well that this may be our last Christmas together, I still feel it will be the sweetest yet. Who can tell just *which* of us will not be here next year—yet to us our joy in Christ will overtake *any* sorrow.
  "When thou passeth through the waters, I will be with thee and through the rivers, they shall not overflow thee . . ." (Isaiah 43:2 KJV).
  Merry Christmas, dear Mother. I love you very much.
                                                                JOYCE

(Actually, it did turn out to be her last Christmas.)

Little did I dream, in my blissfully ignorant sincerity, that she would react to my card exactly as if she had just run barefoot over several hundred sharp tacks. She flew at me from every direction—phone, letters, and in person! She was as mad as a wet hen that I would insinuate she was not well or extremely healthy. I could scarcely have foreseen that my words would cause such an emotional fury—but they did! Over and over again she hotly denied she was sick.

I believe it was Sigmund Freud who felt most people wanted to avoid death so much they developed a basic dishonesty toward it. Seeing my ultrahonest and direct mother developing this type of dishonesty was unthinkable to me!

To cap this time of denial in her life, she received another letter. It was from her dear friend Dale Evans Rogers. Dale's accomplishments in show business are well known to everyone, but to my mother Dale was simply a most dear friend. They were co-workers in a Christian sorority in the San Fernando Valley. They saw each other quite often, but during this time of my mother's illness Dale had been out of town. She was on her usual hectic schedule, but someone had finally told her of my mother's surgery and of the malignancy of the tumors.

Dale, absolutely no stranger to death and dying—having lost her daughters Robin and Debbie—wrote my mother a letter right out of her heart. She said she'd just learned of my mother having cancer. (Whoops—that turned out to be Dale's first mistake.) Then she talked about how wonderful it would be for Mother to soon be with our Lord. (I can just see Mother's reaction as she read *that* line.) Then Dale, because her own acceptance of death was so real, alive, and well adjusted, said she wished she could go to heaven with Mother. Dale told of her children already with the Lord and how she longed to see them. She ended by writing in her own poetic style of beauty that she wished Mother could take her with her when she went. I thought it was the most meaningful and beautiful letter I'd ever read in my life. My mother's reaction to Dale's letter was just the opposite. She was furious.

It was one of the few times anything about death was funny, because there my mother lay in bed, too sick to be up and about, with my letter and Dale's in her hand, bawling me out to a tee for even thinking "such thoughts." Her deep brown black eyes were just snapping as she scolded me and I remember thinking, "For one who is *so* sick the old darling's got a lot of fight left in her." I never loved her more, but I knew so little about the ways of denial I was no help to her.

I wish I'd known denial is usually a temporary state of mind. At least I wish I'd known that it tends to come and go after it once starts in the terminally ill.

During the next few months Mother laid her denial aside briefly and only in rare moments, especially if she felt sick. But as soon as she felt better her confidence of recovery would increase and she would resume her denial.

Much later, when she was not responding to chemotherapy or cobalt treatments and lumps had formed on the other breast, she quietly put down her denial. She began to fortify herself by working out with the weights of acceptance. It was back-breakingly hard. But it paid off and we were to see (and be amazed at) the refinement dying gave to the quality of her mind and soul.

I had not, early in her illness, experienced the real rugged pain of death denial in my own mind. At first it simply did not occur to me she would die *in* surgery so I didn't give any time to it. After surgery, when the diagnosis of cancer was given, I began to be preoccupied with helping Mother to see her denial.

I remember that I was caught up in the general feeling that denial was totally bad and an extremely weak character trait. I was pretty proud and self-righteous about my ability to face things head-on. Such thinking set me up very well for the hard fall later.

I now know that denial is needed in our emotions to act as a buffer or safety zone after we see the reality of someone else's (or our own) death. It gives our ravaged soul a time to draw back and rest a bit. It gives a temporary measure of healing. It can be used in our lives as a God-given diversion.

Somewhere along the line we as Christians have been given the general feeling that if you are a Christian denial is not a problem or, in some cases, shouldn't even exist. What happens then when a Christian *does* experience denial? And what if, in his denial, his actions do not appear to be too Christian? What does he do with the guilt that this produces?

I remember a fantastic woman of God who talked with me many months after her daughter was killed in an automobile accident.

Her daughter, Beck, had left to go to her job in a neighboring town, and at what she thought was a four-way stop, had pulled out in front of a cement truck. The truck hit her car—Beck was thrown out—and the truck crushed her, instantly, into God's presence.

Her mother sat across the table from me during one of my luncheon engagements. "What upsets me most," she said, "is that when I was told Beck was dead, I did a horrible thing."

"What horrible thing?" I asked.

"Well, you know. Christians are supposed to be calm and say nice Scripture verses. I didn't. I got hysterical. Why wasn't I able to be like the wife of one of those missionaries who were killed by the Auca Indians of Ecuador? When Betty Saint heard her husband was dead, she quoted Romans 8:28. ['All things work together for good to them that love God, to them who are the called according to his purpose' KJV.] She *acted* like a Christian."

I was burning with shame for myself and for any other Christian who had ever set up such false standards for Christians. Here was a mother reacting to the sudden death of her daughter in a most normal, human way, yet we the churchpeople, the Christians, had set up phony goals which created her enormous guilt.

"First of all," I began, "let's talk about the missionary's wife. She knew, before her husband and the other four missionaries left on that airplane, that they were about to make contact with men who were part of a well-known headhunter's tribe. The danger was real and the risk enormous.

"In your case, though, you had no such risk attached to saying good-bye to Beck that day. There was nothing to indicate it would be anything but a routine trip to work.

"Secondly, back to the missionaries—the first radio transmission they missed indicated trouble. By the second, and then the third, at half-hour intervals, there was not much doubt that serious trouble had ensued. The wives were, at that point, dealing with their denial and God was giving them the death knowledge very gradually to help their acceptance. It is not any surprise, knowing the caliber of these dedicated men and women and understanding the dangerous risks involved, that when the dreaded message finally came, these women had passed through the early denial and had progressed to a God-given acceptance and were able by God's strength to quote Romans 8.

"You, on the other hand, had no such series of warnings. You were not mercifully granted the death knowledge gradually. Your denial took the form of hysterics and it has nothing to do with whether you were a strong Christian or a weak one."

"Sudden death," as Stephanie, the young widow, told me, "was easy on John but hard on me."

We need denial to help us through the most shocking moments of our painful knowledge.

When I was talking with Dr. White about denial, the sudden-death denial problem came up. He told me of a young boy and his mother.

The boy had been hit by a car while riding a motorcycle. He was rushed to the hospital where Dr. White happened to be on duty in the emergency room. The boy was dead on arrival.

Then the boy's mother was contacted where she worked and told her son had been in an accident. She left work and hurried to the hospital. Even as she entered the emergency entrance her system was getting ready for any bad news she might hear. The beginning of denial was activated.

Doctor White met her in the hall and he helped prepare her by telling her as much as he knew about the actual accident itself. He did *not* tell her the boy was dead. He then told the mother about the injuries—"broken arm, possible heavy internal bleeding and head and body cuts." Then he left her in the hall to give her a chance to digest what she had just heard.

It is too much to ask of a human being to be hit with "sudden death" news all in one blow. (That is why my friend had such hysterics over her daughter Beck's death.)

By leaving the mother, even for just moments, he was gently letting her assimilate his grievous message.

In a few minutes, Dr. White came back and said, "It is not going well." He explained what they had done medically and what emergency treatments and procedures had been used.

Even if a patient arrives dead, most doctors immediately use all the emergency treatments and drugs available to try to continue life, if at all possible. Sometimes the dead-on-arrival verdict has been reversed and a life has been medically resurrected because of their efforts so they try everything.

They used oxygen and heart massage so Dr. White told the mother about it in detail, and then he ended with, "Now we have done everything we could possibly do." Once more he left the mother so his words would do their work of preparation.

When he came back, the mother had been joined by the anxious father and Dr. White led both of them down a corridor and into a small private examining room. All of this had taken only a few minutes, but it was desperately needed.

Doctor White said to me, "Even as we walked toward the room both the mother and father already sensed their son was dead."

When they reached the room, Dr. White said, "We did all we could to save him, but we couldn't. He is gone."

He had just confirmed what they had "known" for the last few minutes and what they'd hoped was not true.

The doctor had told no lies, but he had withheld the information just a few minutes to let the mother prepare herself. This is exactly the same procedure as in the case of a patient just out of surgery. The doctor withholds his information ever so temporarily so the patient's emotions and physical well-being are not immediately jeopardized.

The mother's sobbing broke the tension in the room as she buried her face into her husband's shoulder. Even though her voice was muffled, we can hear the agony of her soul as she said, "Oh, no."

This is the exact moment that being a Christian really counts. We are not removed from denial just because we are God's children, but we should know and recognize denial for what it is.

We should use denial as it is intended, as a buffer zone, and then move into acceptance. We must not live in denial. Anyone who tries to escape the realities of life and death will not be able to handle the ways of death and dying.

It is sad to see someone who has never moved out of denial into acceptance, such as a father I know who was very close to his teenage son. After the son died of leukemia the father refused to go to football games. He treated that sport as a sacred memory to his son. He allowed no games on TV, nor did he ever talk sports with anyone, and by doing so he kept denial alive.

Then there is a widow I know who refuses to touch her dead husband's things. She keeps his den closed just exactly as he left it. She has left his car as he left it—refusing to take out his paper and trash on the front seat. She is committing mental suicide.

Both the grieving father and widow I've just described are Christians, yet they are letting their fears of death and the fierce desire to deny death rob them of having any real relationships with people who *are* alive. This type of denial is very hard on families and friends and its frustrations severely strain communications between them. It also, most certainly, renders them ineffective in living the abundant life God has promised.

If we are to move out of denial toward acceptance, it will not be easy. It will not be without its cost and complications. But if we look closely, we see it's a very old problem.

Jesus tried so hard to help His disciples over the hurdles of denial. He told them, repeatedly, that He would be betrayed and would be crucified, but they covered their hearts and minds with the robes of denial. Not too long before His death Mary, the sister of Martha, poured a very expensive perfume over Jesus' head. The disciples, blinded by denial, missed the whole point of her selfless act. They were indignant because the woman had wasted so much money. They were full of suggestions about how she could have sold the perfume and spent the money on the poor.

Jesus simply told them they would always have the poor. Then He reminded them of His upcoming death and said (again) that they would not always have Him.

Then, verbally, Jesus painted a beautiful picture of a woman who had passed denial and moved into acceptance—and at great cost —when He said, "She has done what she could, and has anointed my body ahead of time for burial" (Mark 14:8).

A doctor specializing in leukemia found in children gave the chilling statistics that 70 percent of the parents obtain a divorce once leukemia has been diagnosed in their child. He also stated if parents and family *accepted* and recognized the confirmed diagnosis of leukemia, they responded by trying to prepare themselves for the extreme burdens of caring for their sick child. They answered their other children's questions straight on and they helped the child himself to know he was loved and not being dropped or abandoned because he had this disease. They were with the child when he died. However, the story was sadly different for parents who denied the diagnosis and the final, terminal end of the disease. The stress of this denial usually produced, if not divorce, a separation, and ultimately kept them away from the hospital when death was imminent.

I was shocked and saddened to learn that in one of our major children's hospitals near us many babies and children die without either parent, doctor, or nurse being present. They die alone because

parents and professional people do not want to get emotionally
involved with a bound-to-die child. They die alone because adults
deny death for fear of the hurt they might experience after the
child has died.

Nurses carry out their various duties with callous indifference.
They listen as little as possible and touch only when necessary. How
sad, but such is the *force* of denial.

It's as if they do indeed hear the mourning song, but they run
blindly from the sound, holding their ears as they run and hoping
none of the message will get through their carefully structured
blockades.

I have seen the terminally ill children in several hospitals and I
can fully appreciate how soul-tearing it is to try and work around
them. However, it still is tragic to let denial rob us of feeling, caring, and loving the dying child.

My co-worker, Dr. James Dobson, told me of a mother who was
willing to put down her denial, pick up her *own* acceptance, and
then beautifully prepare her little son for his death.

She was a large, black woman, as picturesque as the plantation
mammies of years ago. She came every day to the hospital to visit
her little five-year-old son who was dying of the painful disease
lung cancer.

One morning, before the mother got there, a nurse heard the
little boy saying, "I hear the bells! I hear the bells! They're ringing!"
Over and over that morning nurses and staff heard him.

When the mother arrived she asked one of the nurses how her
son had been that day, and the nurse replied, "Oh, he's hallucinating today—it's probably the medication, but he's not making any
sense. He keeps on saying he hears bells."

Then that beautiful mother's face came alive with understanding,
and she shook her finger at the nurse and said, "You listen to me.
He is *not* hallucinating and he's not out of his head because of any
medicine. I told him weeks ago that when the pain in his chest got
bad and it was hard to breathe, it meant he was going to leave us.
It meant he was going to go to heaven—and that when the pain got
really bad he was to look up into the corner of his room—towards
heaven—and listen for the bells of heaven—*because they'd be ringing for him!*" With that, she marched down that hall, swept into

her little son's room, swooped him out of his bed, and rocked him in her arms until the sounds of ringing bells were only quiet echoes, and he was gone.

I see her in my mind's eye—a mother who had undoubtedly experienced denial, but she was not about to wallow in it herself or delude her child with it. She had rocked her son into the arms of God—with both of them knowing the peace of acceptance, and both of them hearing the mourning song.

We need denial—but we must not linger in it. We must recognize it as one of God's most unique tools and use it. Denial is our special oxygen mask to use when the breathtaking news of death has sucked every ounce of air out of us. It facilitates our bursting lungs by giving them their first gulps of sorrow-free air. We breathe in the breath of denial and it seems to maintain life. We do not need to feel guilty or judge our level of Christianity for clutching the mask to our mouth. However, after breathing has been restored and the initial danger has passed, we need not be dependent on it.

I think God longs for us to lay down the oxygen mask of denial, and with His help begin breathing into our lungs the fresh, free air of acceptance *on our own.*

4

A Time for Anger

There is a right time for everything:
A time to be born,
A time to die;
A time to lose;
A time to speak up;
A time for hating.
ECCLESIASTES 3:1, 2, 6, 7, 8

For some years now I have been writing down, here and there, incidents or feelings of the moment. I have done so without the thought of publishing. I wrote merely as a therapeutic release exercise and as a record to jog my memory lapses from time to time.

More than once in a while I did not understand my moods or reactions, but I jotted them down anyway just as they hit me. As I reread these notes, I find that some are remarkably complete and others are rather sketchy. Still others have been done in a kind of ridiculous shorthand and are highly indecipherable. I suppose somewhere, in the back roads of my mind, I envisioned a future time when I'd reexamine the words and come up with some reasonable explanations.

One rather complete set of notes was written one night after a funeral. I'd been overwhelmed by anger and these were my thoughts, as I wrote them.

Everything about our mortuary is carefully geared to comfort the grieving families and friends of the deceased. Why doesn't it work on me?

The main chapel with its Spanish-Moorish decor has curved, arched windows and doorways instead of sharp, angular abutments and they all blend into a tolerable softness.

The carpeting is a warm sage green and the beige walls are decorated with elaborately scrolled, wrought iron sconces. Their golden bulbs cast a small, warm glow over the walls and the thick velvet drapes.

The pews are richly carved wood with padded seats and they lend a source of solid security to the hall. In fact, over the whole place is the light fragrance of stability and security. It's all been planned and designed to bring words like "peace" and "acceptance" into meaningful focus.

It's all been wasted on me because not only did I *not* have peace or acceptance this morning, I found I had tensed up at a pretty fast rate of speed.

I was late getting there so I stood with the overflow crowd in the vestibule. For a long time I looked through the windows into the beautifully appointed chapel and down the aisle at the flag-draped casket of my friend. When I could bear that scene no longer, I began concentrating on the beauty of the flowers. Some flowers had been placed in their containers by hands trained in mechanical precision—they looked very dead, plastic, or both. Others were tenderly arranged with sensitive, talented hands and, even from where I stood, the results were breathtaking. They reminded me of life and the land of the living. They seemed to bring my heart a small measure of comfort, but I grew restless again with a growing sense of anxiety. To make time move, I looked up to study the ceiling. Large chandeliers were hung by delicately worked, yet strong, black chains. They were masterpieces of old-world design. Their filigreed iron cylinders framed the amber-colored glass panels and the small light inside glowed with warmth and charm. Still, they did not ease my tension.

Finally, our minister stepped to the small lectern and I gave him my full effort of concentration. His message was not merely appropriate, it was a masterpiece of rhetoric, held together by truth and *right*ness. At one place he said, "John would not want to come back now, not after seeing what he's now seen—not after hearing what he has now heard and not now, after knowing what he now knows!"

Even understanding the truth of his words and believing them with all my heart did not seem to help. Maybe part of my uneasiness is that sometimes there is a quality of dishonest phoniness, hypocrisy, at a funeral. It can get out of hand. Too many nice, rather untrue, things are said about the deceased. Too many tears shed for someone we hardly spoke to in life. Too much evading of the truth. Like this morning. The organist was just terrible, but we said, "Wasn't the music lovely." However, the soloist was good and his song echoed majestically through a screen into the chapel and out to those of us in the lobby, but my heart was still not comforted.

There was, by now, no slight feeling of anxiety, but rather an electric current of frustration jabbing here and there at my soul. I could feel myself getting angry. In fact, by the time I passed by the side door I was stinging with resentments and anger.

Just outside the door two of the morticians recognized me (I've been the guest soloist there for many funerals), smiled, and said hello. I was so bent out of shape over the utterly abhorrent devastation death does to the living I barely muttered hello as I brushed past them. It's not like me to be so rude.

All day long I've been angry. In John's case, death came and robbed him of his life. Then, not content with what he did to John, death hovers over John's wife and children with a sinister smile that simply infuriates me!

No beautiful chapel, flowers, sermon, or song seem to appease or comfort me. I'm mad at everybody—from God on down to the guys who are covering up John's casket right now.

It was much later, after I'd written these jumbled thoughts, that I read about anger in Dr. Kübler-Ross's book and a little bell rang, signaling the beginning of some understanding.

As surely as denial is our first reaction to death, just as surely it is followed by anger. Denial moves into anger, especially in the terminally ill, because reality of dying becomes too evident to deny. Their attitude goes from, "Oh, no—not me," to, "Oh, yes," then to "Why me?" It seems perfectly logical to warm up the cold atmosphere of death by the heat of anger.

Aside from the sporadic anger I experienced at John's funeral, my first real bout with anger emerged one hour after our baby David had died.

I have told in *His Stubborn Love* of the beautiful moments just after my husband told me David had died. The presence of God simply sustained us in an incredible way, but I did not write of the hours that followed later because I felt guilty about them. I did not know that being angry over your loss was normal or that the anger would pass. I could not write of those angry thoughts then because I thought Christians were not to have them.

As my husband told me of David's death, a nurse gave me a shot. It did not put me out, it just took the edge off reality and put me under a bit. Dick stayed with me for a little while and then he felt if he went home I would get a better rest, so he tearfully kissed me good-bye.

It seemed that as he left, so did the tranquil presence of God. I became fearful as I thought God had left, too. I knew fear, combined with loneliness, had climbed over the rails of my bed and when I wasn't looking anger slipped under the covers with them. Dick had been gone only a few minutes when a doctor banged through my door, shook my bed, and shoved some papers on a clipboard in my face. I thought he said, "Here, sign this." I was so far under because of the tranquilizer by then that I couldn't hear him too well. I asked him what he said and he repeated it.

"What is it for?" I asked.

"It's permission to do an autopsy."

With angry, stinging tears pouring down my face, I signed it with the most ridiculous scrawl I'd ever written. He left immediately without a word.

I knew enough about the immense value of autopsies to know that I wanted it done. (David died of internal hemorrhaging due to the Rh-negative blood problem. Today, just eight years later, babies do not die from those complications. In part, autopsies were responsible for helping doctors find the treatment and cure for this problem. But having it so crudely and abruptly shoved into my face seemed unnecessarily cruel.)

About then the loss of my little son began to be real. It had happened. The song of mourning was rising to a deafening fortissimo in my ears. It was as if the music had been written and orchestrated only for the percussion instruments and everything was pounding, striking, or clanging together. The only lyrics I could come up with were, "Lord, why did You do that?"

Someone, somewhere inside of me, seemed to be beating out a slow, throbbing rhythm on the tympani drums and the pulsing sounded like the ugly word *dead*. "Dead—dead—dead—"

I wanted to scream, "Stop this horrid music—stop it or I will burst with these hideous, noisy sounds."

I knew then—for sure—I'd leave the hospital with an armful of azalea plants, but no baby. Hot tears seared and stung my eyes. I was still crying when a nurse from the baby nursery strode into my room. She took one look at me, put her hands on her hips, and said, "You're not ready! Why aren't you ready? You know the procedure. Why aren't you washed and ready?"

"Ready for what?" I mumbled. She threw her hands up in a what-am-I-gonna-do-with-them gesture, looked at her watch, and said, "It's 4:30 and time for you to nurse your baby. You signed up to nurse—now the babies are coming out—you got the sheet of instructions—why aren't you ready?"

I looked up at her for a couple of seconds and, as steady as I could, I said very slowly, "My baby is dead."

"Oh! *Oh!*" she said, and vanished. Somehow she missed the other nurse from the nursery because it was a second or two later when another nurse, two babies in her arms, stuck her head in my room and said, "Mrs. Landorf, are you ready?"

"No, I'm not. My—" She cut me off with, "Oh, come on—hurry up."

"My baby is dead." It hurt to put it into words the first time, but saying it again almost gagged me.

"My heavens, Mrs. Landorf, they don't tell us anything around here. I'm sorry."

I wasn't mad at her, but at the whole mess in general. I nodded and smiled a half smile and looked at the tiny little bundles in her arms. They were beautiful *but*—they were someone else's.

The next nurse entered my room with a baby on one arm. She passed my bed without a look in my direction and settled my roommate's baby down into his mother's bed.

I'll never forget the sounds of that room so long as I live. The mother was saying all those dear, unintelligible things one coos over her infant as he nurses and it ravaged my heart. The baby's contented sucking sounds and little moans of joy came across the room as if they were being miked into loudspeakers above my bed. I felt as if all the life in me was being crushed out.

The beautiful presence of God that had been so strong, so comforting less than an hour ago was gone. Dick was gone. David was gone. I kept wondering why God had chosen this very moment to go, too. I was alone. I felt exactly as if some mysterious plague had wiped out every living being on the face of the earth.

Someone at the head desk got very busy all of a sudden and in a swish of activity my roommate, bed, and baby were moved out. Then I really was alone.

At that moment a minister I know stuck his head in my door and said a cheerful hi. I was pleased to see him, but I couldn't set my thoughts straight because I was still very angry. I was rather quiet. The minister did not seem to notice. He just patted my shoulder and with a confident smile said, "Well now, Joyce, you have this thing under control—don't you? You have no problems with your baby's death, do you?"

He blew my mind right off its hinges. I thought, "No problems! Are you insane? One hour ago my baby died. Since then I've been to hell and back—I'm just out of surgery, I think I'm dying, and I'm so mad at God I can hardly see straight and you are smugly confident I have no problems. How dare you assume I am such a strong Christian and have no problems?"

Then the old bugaboo about "What will people think of me—or my image?" took effect. I realized this minister had put me up on a spiritual pedestal. I was not supposed to have any hang-ups over death because my name was Joyce Landorf. I didn't want to blow my image, so I lied.

I looked him in the eye and mouthed the lie: "Oh, no problems at all. My baby is with the Lord and everything is all right."

It was the answer he was counting on so he patted my shoulder again and said, "Good girl." Then he slipped quietly out of my room so I could sleep. As soon as he was gone I picked up a glass vase, thought better of it, and did not shatter it against the closed door.

Why did I lie to him? Why didn't I tell him I was angry? The guilt I felt for feeling anger, in the first place, and lying, in the second place, was painfully thumping against my mind.

It was not until just a few years ago that C. S. Lewis, in his book *A Grief Observed*, explained that day of anger for me. He was describing a woman who lost her child as being made in two parts. She had a "God-aimed eternal spirit" side and a motherhood side.

He talked of God being a comfort and a hope to her "God-aimed" spirit side, but not to her motherhood side. He said, "The specifically maternal happiness must be written off. Never, in any place or time, will she have her son on her knees, or bathe him, or tell him a story, or plan his future, or see her grandchild."

It seemed an extraordinary miracle of understanding broke inside of me as I read those words.

I am made in two parts. One responds to God and to His touch on my life. I love Him. I trust Him and know—no matter how loused up my world may be—He is in control of me and my little world. My baby is not suffering. My baby is well, warm, and is being rocked to sleep in the arms of God. With this whole side I respond to God's restoration of my soul. I experience an unexplainable, uncanny peace. I can begin the difficult task of accepting death. Spiritually, I am satisfied, filled to the brim of me by the unexhaustible source of God's love.

The other part of me? Ah, now, that's a different story. The human side, the earthly, feet-on-the-ground part of me, the motherhood in me—all of this side is *not* comforted. Not by a long shot. Am I less a Christian? No! I am just more a mother-human being at this point. My dreams are broken. My plans, even the one to be a great mother to this child now that I'm a Christian, are cancelled. I can have no more babies. I have to move, walk, and live in a world where other babies live on. I have to go back to home and church to face my friend Shirley and her baby. Her son—born at the same time, the same hospital, and three rooms away. Her son who lives. I am not ready or willing to do this. I am angry and wonder over and over, "Why *my* baby?" Seeing the hopelessly ill and suffering babies at Children's Hospital should put things in a different perspective, to give some measure of relief, but it doesn't. I just want *my* baby.

"Oh," you say, "but just think—David is with the Lord!" My

mother-self rises up and screams out with inescapable anger, "Well, you tell the Lord to give him back to me. I want him in my arms, not God's." The human side is experiencing the normal emotion of anger.

One mother, whose son died of bone cancer on his sixteenth birthday, described her bout with anger as her son lay dying. She said that early in her son's illness the Lord had plainly told her that her son (named David, too) would not live. She had at that moment begun preparing herself for his death. As the illness drew toward the end, friends came to the hospital to visit the boy. Over and over again they would talk briefly with the boy and then go out into the hall and break down in tears. The boy's mother would put her arms around them and tenderly she'd comfort *them*.

Many times after she'd soothed her friends' heartache they would ask her how she held up—and how could she be so cheerful and helpful?

She said her answer was the same: "Of course I don't want David to die. But he *is* going to. I'm smiling and able to understand the finality of his going, but inside I'm yelling, '———! He's my beautiful son,' and the mother in me wants him to live!"

She confessed to me that while she loved God with all her heart, and swearing was not in her vocabulary, it was the only way that was adequate to express her rage. She felt a little guilty about this and yet it was the only thing that fit the situation.

I can well understand her mother-type anger. Later, after my mother died, one well-meaning Christian lady wrote, "Always remember, your mother went to be with her Lord. She is probably much happier now."

In the margin of that note I'd furiously scrawled, *But I'm not!* The daughter-side of me was reacting with considerable anger.

In another letter received at that same time, my friend Bobbie had written, "Just heard of your loss. No matter how you are prepared—losing a mother is never easy!"

In the margin of her letter I wrote, *Right!* Bobbie had understood the daughter-side of me very well!

One widow told me several Christians said, in saccharine-sweet tones, "Don't worry, God never takes something away without giving you something better." The widow said she kept wanting to scream, "Are you kidding? My husband was the best—the very best!" She was angry at the thoughtlessness of people and her wife-side recoiled every time she heard this trite comment.

Joe Bayly's father-side was angry when he wrote of his eighteen-year-old son's death. I'm terribly grateful for his angry honesty. Joe's books and writings have stirred me and many others to action. He has uplifted my spiritual side to God many times, but the day I read his psalm in *Psalms of My Life* about his son, I learned all about Joe Bayly—the father.

A Psalm on the Death of an 18-Year-Old Son

What waste Lord
this ointment precious
here outpoured
is treasure great
beyond my mind to think.
For years
until this midnight
it was safe
contained
awaiting careful use
now broken
wasted
lost.
The world is poor
so poor it needs each drop
of such a store.
This treasure spent
might feed a multitude
for all their days
and then yield more.
This world is poor?
It's poorer now
the treasure's lost.
I breathe its lingering fragrance
soon even that
will cease.
What purpose served?
The act is void of reason
sense

madmen do such deeds
not sane.
The sane man hoards his treasure
spends with care
if good
to feed the poor
or else to feed himself.
Let me alone Lord
You've taken from me
what I'd give Your world.
I cannot see
such waste
that You should take
what poor men need.
You have a heaven
full of treasure
could You not wait
to exercise Your claim
on this?
O spare me Lord forgive
that I may see
beyond this world
beyond myself
Your sovereign plan
or seeing not
may trust You
Spoiler of my treasure.
Have mercy Lord
here is my quitclaim.

Anger and the frustrating resentments in and about death are so annihilating few of us can admit it, much less cope with it.

If we can somehow admit to our anger, either verbally to a close friend or in writing, as Joe Bayly has, there comes a *small* amount of healing.

I think the loudest crescendo point of my angry mourning song was reached in my life the day of our son's funeral.

I was still in the hospital recovering from major surgery so the morning of David's funeral I said to my husband, "Now, as soon as the service is over please call me from the mortuary and tell me all about it." It was to be a private memorial for our son. We invited both sets of grandparents, two couples who were dear friends of ours, and of course our children, Laurie and Rick.

I lay in the hospital, feeling very small and lonely, but I had asked the head nurse to see to it that no one bothered me at 10:00 A.M. because I did want to be alone. In view of the other mishaps over David's death, they were eager to cooperate and mercifully I was left to tend my own wounds.

About 10:45, my phone rang and my husband gave me a running account of the service and all that happened. Laurie and Rick had responded well to Dr. Ted Cole's brief message and Laurie had come prepared to cry with carefully folded tissues clutched in her little hands. Near the end of Dick's recounting he said, a little hesitantly, "There is one thing, honey, you should know." When I asked what, he said very slowly, "Your parents didn't come."

As soon as I said good-bye to him, with my heart racing and pounding nearly out of my chest, I called my parents' home.

My dad answered and when he asked, "How are you today?" I just incredulously cried, "Dad, how come you and Mother weren't at David's funeral? How come you weren't there?" I said it over several times as if to convince my own self it *was* a valid question. Had they really *not* come?

"Oh, honey," he laughed a bit, "we didn't think it was so very important. He was just a baby."

"Just a baby?" My mind instantly froze in unbelief—"No he wasn't *just any* baby—he was your grandson!" By then my mother picked up the other extension and asked what was wrong. I told her and quickly she responded with, "Oh, honey, we are so sorry." My dad added his words—"Yes, we are sorry, honey—but you didn't need me in a ministerial capacity—you had Dr. Ted."

"I *know* I had Dr. Ted," I shouted, "but I needed you! You are David's grandparents." My dad said something about my sister having a dental appointment that day, but the percussion instruments in my head were clobbering me with their deafening noise and what was said next was drowned out.

In the end I was crying, Dad was crying, Mother was crying, and if the operator had been listening, she would have been crying, too, as we all said, "I'm so sorry" over and over again.

I will always remember replacing the receiver on the phone. It was an incredible experience.

My folks had not bothered to come to their grandson's funeral. They were sorry and had asked for my forgiveness. I *said*, "Yes, of course I forgive you," but how come when the phone call ended and I lay back on my pillows my anger was just beginning to really hit and I was nowhere near forgiveness toward them?

Thirty minutes later, by the time my husband arrived, I was vomiting. He called the nurse and she called the doctor. I was given a sedative but within three hours a bladder infection erupted and my stay in the hospital was increased by five more pain-filled days.

I could not understand all that was happening. I had *said*, "I forgive you" to my parents, but why hadn't my body or my emotions accepted it? Everything inside me was glistening with angry fervor and, try as I may, I could *not* forgive totally and I knew I'd never be capable of forgetting. Anger rose swiftly around me and I almost drowned in the mental and physical anguish of it. I kept telling myself I was making too much of the issue, but I countered that it was unreal for my parents not to come to their grandson's funeral. The battle raged within me for days and never have I been so dangerously ill.

When I was finally released, I left the hospital carrying (as I suspected) an azalea plant instead of a baby and still aching with the fever of anger raging inside of me.

It was some months later that I realized the bitterness I felt toward my parents was consuming my mind mentally and corroding my insides physically and something had to be done to stop its devasting effects on my life. I needed to be well and whole in all areas yet every time I saw my parents all I did was silently scream the question, "Why didn't you come?" and for days after their visit I'd be down in bed desperately ill again.

One day I finally leveled with the Lord. I said, "I'm sorry, Lord (whenever we say it like that, chances are we are not *too* terribly sorry!), but there's *no way* I can forgive my parents. You know I've tried, but I can't explain their absence at the funeral to Dick's parents, our friends, or our children, much less to myself. I *cannot* forgive them!"

I'll never forget the quiet, still, small voice that spoke in my living room that day. The Lord said, *I know* you *can't forgive them—I made you—I know your limitations—I know you are unable to really forgive them.* But I can *so let Me.*

The angry, pounding music stopped for a bit—or maybe it just eased and quieted down—but positively I heard a soft, gentle melody beginning somewhere outside my room. Did I dare hope?

"Lord," I questioned, "how can You forgive so I'll feel a release from this angry bitterness?"

My child, He answered, *let Me simply channel My forgiveness through you. Open your heart and mind to Me. Do not try to forgive them on your own. I'll do it* through you. *It will be* My *work—not yours.*

I'm not sure, even at this moment, how I opened up my heart and mind but some way, somehow, when you're desperate you *find* the way so I opened up all the secret cupboards of my soul. It was my first moment of quiet peace since that disturbing phone call so many months before. A song of freedom rang through my heart and mind and I breathed in its beautiful message.

A few days later, when I saw my parents, I realized I'd been with them two hours and had not once thought of the anguishing day of David's funeral. It felt marvelous to stand back—relax—and let God forgive where I couldn't!

A few months after experiencing God's forgiveness in my anger and one year later, to the day, of David's funeral, my aunt called to tell us my Grandpa Uzon had died. I left our home that morning and drove to their house to see what I could do for Grandma or my aunt.

I found Grandma in her little house built behind my aunt's, standing in her living room. She was just standing there shaking her head in disbelief.

My grandfather had not only been her husband for over fifty years, but her ears as well.

They had come to America from Hungary when they were in their late twenties, bringing with them my mother, Marion, and her brother, Peter. Not long after they settled into a newly built house, my grandmother had caught cold from the still-damp plastered walls, and it had left her completely deaf.

Grandpa became her newspaper reader, her chief interpreter, her radio listener, her TV explainer, her Bible reader, and main hymn singer.

The night before he died, Grandpa had (as usual) read the Scriptures out of their big Hungarian Bible. She had joyously followed his lips with her eyes. It was the most happy part of their day. Then he sang the old gospel song, "My Heavenly Father Watches Over Me." She ran her fingers across the words in the hymnal. It was their special, private time with each other and with God.

Later they went to bed and Grandpa gave the little night table between their beds two quick shoves, bumping it against Grandma's bed. It was his good-night signal. She leaned up a bit, looked over at him, and he responded by blowing two kisses to her. She elaborately caught them and settled down to sleep.

To wake early the next morning and wonder why his bed was empty, only to be told he'd gotten up, awakened my aunt in the front house, and died while he waited in the living room for help—could not be true. She had missed it all. She had said no good-byes.

A few hours later when I got there, all she said when she saw me was, "Papa gone—Papa go."

When I found one of my uncles was flying in from the East and staying at Grandma's house, I decided to make myself useful and get the bedroom ready. Grandma quietly followed me.

I took the sheets off Grandpa's bed first. I wasn't too sure exactly where the soiled laundry went, so by a look I shot the question of "Where do these go?" to Grandma. She nodded her head in her direction, so I tossed the sheets to her. The sheets were midair when she realized exactly what she was catching—and why. Disbelief settled over her face and quickly resolved into anger. She caught the sheets, held them very close, and with her eyes just snapping, she stamped her foot ever so lightly and said, "Oh, Papa, vy you go and not take me? Huh? Vy?"

She was even madder nine months later at my mother's funeral. She had resigned herself to my mother's dying in the last days of my mother's illness and had done quite well until just *after* the funeral when the family was saying their final good-byes.

I saw her standing, bending over my mother's casket, and fairly hissing a verbal stream of Hungarian downward. When she saw me, she stood up and switched to her fractured English. Pointing at my mother, she said, "*She* was not go. I next." She held up one finger to me—"Papa," she said. Then, the second finger—"Me." And with the third finger pointing to my mother's casket, she said, "*Then* Marion."

Then she turned from me and looked down at my mother, bent over her, whispered something in her ear, kissed her cheek, and said, "To Jesus."

I thought she was over her mad, but as Grandma passed me she muttered under her breath, "I seventy-nine year. Time me go, not your mama."

Knowing she was free to express her anger to me and others in the family, including my mother, brought Grandma her measure of healing. However, she stayed just a little mad at God for the next six years over this until He finally told her it was her turn to go.

At the beginning of this chapter I quoted the Old Testament about having a time for everything. When we become involved directly (or indirectly) with death and dying, there is a time for doubts, frustrations, and anger, but there also is a time for healing, for faith, and for understanding.

We know that time heals all wounds—or does it? How can we help those during their time in the intensive-care wards of sorrow? How can I—as a friend, a daughter, a wife, a mother—hurry up the recovery time of a person in anger?

After Job, in the Old Testament, had lost all his children, stock, land, everything, he had three friends come to visit him. They were full of advice. At one point Job pleaded with them and said, "Let me be free to speak out of the bitterness of my soul" (Job 7:11). One of his friends impatiently snapped back, "How long will you go on like this, Job, blowing words around like wind?" (Job 8:2). Later, completely exasperated, Job said, "I am weary of living. Let me complain freely. I will speak in my sorrow and bitterness" (Job 10:1).

I don't want to be a "Job's friend" to anyone experiencing the frustrations of death and dying. I read Dorothy Parker's poem and thought for a long time about what kind of friend I'd try to be.

The False Friends

They laid their hands upon my head,
They stroked my cheek and brow;
And time could heal a hurt, they said,
And time could dim a vow.

And they were pitiful and mild
Who whispered to me then,
"The heart that breaks in April, child,
Will mend in May again."

Oh, many a mended heart they knew,
So old they were, and wise.
And little did they have to do
To come to me with lies!

Who flings me silly talk of May
Shall meet a bitter soul;
For June was nearly spent away
Before my heart was whole.

I must treat the broken hearts I find with gentle, loving respect.
I must let them "complain freely."

Peter wrote so long ago, "And now this word to all of you: You
should be like one big happy family, full of sympathy toward each
other, loving one another with tender hearts and humble minds"
(1 Peter 3:8).

Today I looked closely at a man named Thomas—but I looked
even closer at his friends. I found they were "full of sympathy"
toward Thomas and they loved him with "tender hearts and humble
minds."

Do you remember the disciple of Jesus who has been referred to,
over the years, as Doubting Thomas?

I can, in my mind's eye, see him walking along a dirt road to the
house where his associates are gathered. Defiantly, with an angry
fire burning inside him, he kicks a stone out of his way and watches
it as it ricochets off a wall and crushes a small wild flower when it
lands. He feels deceived, betrayed and, if you please, *robbed*. He
trusted someone only to be let down. Just as he had thought he had
found a bona fide person—this man Jesus—who had authority,

power, and the answer to every one of life's problems—this Jesus ends up *dead*. He's executed, murdered, and left nailed on a cross just like any common criminal. Thomas concludes the man was a fraud and now the whole world has seen him die. He arrives at the house at the same time he comes to the summation of his problem and thinks, "I've been had."

He enters the house and angrily lays out his bitterness and anger in front of his friends and fellow workers.

What comes out of that meeting is perfectly beautiful to me.

Thomas's friends do not wash their hands of him—
They do not hush him up and hustle him out a side door—
They do not give him a lecture on the poor quality of spiritual faith
    he seems to be showing—
They do not give him a pat on the back and tell him he'll get over
    this—
They simply say, in great, loving sympathy, "Oh, Thomas, wait until
    you see him!"

How dearly we need to have someone be patient with our doubts, to let us vent our anger, and to understand our frustrations. We need someone not to condemn, challenge, or lecture, but to lovingly help us to wait it out. Someone to turn our eyes on Jesus.

Many months before her death, my mother slipped out of denial into anger. Her angry outburst to me over Dale's letter and my Christmas card was the beginning.

I knew she was moving from, "Oh, no—not me. I don't have cancer," to, "Oh, dear—*it is me*." Since God had been a part of her lifestyle so long, I wondered if her anger would be directed toward Him. I didn't have long to wait.

I was at home one day when I knew I should leave everything and go visit her. So I switched some things around on my calendar and drove the hour or so over to my parents' house. I went down the hall and stuck my head into the den.

There she was in bed, leaning back on the pillows. She had her eyes closed, a smile on her face, and her hands were folded on top of an overturned book.

I remember I didn't even say hello, I just softly asked, "What's happened, sweetie?"

She didn't change her position except to open her eyes to look at me and then she said, "Oh, honey, I've had the most wonderful experience."

She had been reading a book about Dr. Paul Carlson, who was a medical missionary to the Republic of Congo (now Zaire).

She told me she had just gotten to the place where he was running toward the safety of a stone wall when Congolese rebels shot him to death. The area was liberated later, but for him it was just fifteen minutes too late. Mother sat straight up in bed in order to tell it better. She said she had put the book down and felt absolutely furious at God for allowing Dr. Carlson's death. "After all," she told God, "he was only in his thirties—he was a doctor—hard at work for Your cause and for medicine. Why did You do that to him?" she had angrily shouted out to God. "Why did You cut him down in the prime of his life and ministry? What mean joke were You playing on him—to let him go to Africa, be useful, and then have him get shot just as he was about to be safe?"

As I looked at her, she lay back against the pillows and said, with a trace of sweet sorrow touching her voice, "Of course, honey, what I was really downright mad about was why had God allowed me to have such a ministry—and one that was so blessed by His touch—and why was He taking me? Why now?"

It was the first time that I had heard her, in her very own words, admit that she was terminally ill. The moment tore me tenderly apart.

"Don't cry, honey," she said. "Do you know what the Lord answered me about my questions on Dr. Carlson?" (I should have known *He'd* answer her!)

"No—what?" I asked.

"Well, He said, 'Marion, you think Dr. Carlson was busy and effective for Me and My work there in the Congo? Oh, Marion, you should see him *now!*' Then . . . (my mother's eyes were glistening with tears) then, Joyce, the Lord said, 'Marion, my dear child, you think you're busy there? Just wait till you get *here!*'"

It was Victor Hugo who said:

My life has not ended,
I shall begin work again in the morning.

When I read that I remembered the beautiful scene in the den with my mother that day.

She had vocalized her outcry of anger at the Lord. She had recognized it and dealt with it head-on. Though it had taken time, the wounds of anger were clean cuts. The cuts were well on their way to healing because they were not infected with the pus of bitterness or self-pity.

God had not been shocked at her outburst, nor did He punish her for her resentment. He used her anger as an opportunity to give her a hope-filled message. Her past work was not finished, as she thought, but just about to really begin. She could lose her anger within the confines of God's loving message.

She spent her anger that day and I was never to see, hear, or feel anger in her again.

I am so glad our Lord understands our anger at death and dying and I suspect when He was hanging on the cross it was the emotion of anger that fired off the words, "My God, why hast thou forsaken me?"

Anyone who has experienced the agony of dying or those who have stood by the dying have a total band of identity with the anger in Jesus' voice when He said those words.

Jesus' one word *why* in that sentence is the angriest word. We all wonder about the whys of things.

This morning a letter came from a terribly distraught pastor's wife. One line says, "Oh, Joyce, if only God would tell me the whys of this situation. I'd be able to understand it better." But I wonder —would she—would you—would I?

I certainly wish I had some brilliant, illuminating answers to the why of life and death, but I don't. Neither does anybody else.

There is much in life that is complex, contradictory, and certainly above my ability to reason and understand, yet I must go on living. What fascinates me the most is that God seems to give me an appetite for life and satisfies inner hungers many times *without* specific, authoritative answers.

Certainly I do not understand electricity and I'm not too sure

Edison did, either. Electricity is the force which cooks our daily meals—it sustains and maintains life for me and my family. It is the same force which burned the life *out* of a telephone lineman yesterday. I hate the conflict here and I don't pretend to understand the whys, yet I have to live and move on. I must use the electric current in spite of what I know or do not know about its force.

So I do not know the whys of our loved one's death, but I must go on living. I don't enjoy anger, but I must understand it's a natural reflex. I have to hang on by faith and endurance.

Sometimes my faith is stronger than my endurance and in these times God's presence shines like a twenty-five-foot Christmas tree trimmed with one light for every tiny branch. I am dazzled by the sight. Its reflective glow on my face is seen by everyone.

Other times, the lights of faith burn low, flicker, and almost go out. Then I have to hang on to the handle of my endurance. Out of the angry pain of death and dying comes a steadfast, unmovable, but gentle assurance. If I let go, I will surely fall—so I must *hang on*.

Christ was definitely hanging on while He was dying. Yet He gave His own death tremendous dignity. What was—even by its name, *crucifixion*—ugly, gross, violent, and horror-filled, He turned into awesome grandeur. With His bones out of joint, all muscles tearing and burning, and with infectious fever raging out of control, He looked, saw His mother, and delegated John to see to her needs.

Our Lord was angry, He expressed it, but He did not stay in anger. He lovingly took care of others in those moments. Such love, such remarkable love, offset one of the world's ugliest and angriest moments in history.

During a memorial service—on the rim of the Grand Canyon—for the tragic victims of a midair plane collision, an angry young man yelled out, "Where was God when this happened?" The minister in charge of the service asked, "Did everyone hear the question? The young man asked where God was when this life-consuming tragedy happened." Then, for the young man and hundreds of grieving friends and relatives, the minister answered, "God was in the same place He was when cruel men took His only Son and crucified Him on a cross."

We may never know the answers to all the whys or the hows of death, and certainly we may not be able to completely cope with our anger, but God is in command. Someday there will be no anger and no dying, for God will put an end to death forever.

However, until then, *there is a time for anger,* but we must move on, move through it, and move out of its crippling atmosphere.

As Christians we can move out of anger and we can do so without guilty regrets—even when our anger has been directed at God.

We serve a God who understands and we can move, breathe, and live again because of our faith, our God-given endurance, and our heaven-sent hope of everlasting *life.*

5

Striking the Biggest Bargain of All

Spare me, Lord! Let me recover and
be filled with happiness again before
my death.

PSALMS 39.13

My mother was so ill on Christmas Day she hardly moved off the couch except to sit at the dinner table for a few minutes. Yet, somewhere between Christmas Day and the second week of January she experienced a remarkable encounter with God. A fantastic miracle exploded into her life and ours.

She phoned me one rainy day in January, and immediately I was struck by the tone of her voice. She sounded like her old enthusiastic, radiant self and her words just rushed out and tumbled over each other.

"Oh, Joyce, honey, I asked God to heal me and to give me fifteen more years to live. I know God wants me to be healthy and well, so I trusted Him for a complete healing and—" she paused,

77

"He did it! I feel absolutely marvelous!" She finished the sentence with victorious authority ringing in her voice.

My heart took a couple of giant flip-flops and I couldn't find my voice so I didn't respond with anything. I was stunned. The incredible had happened! She had actually bargained with God for a fifteen-year miracle and, by the sound of her voice, I was sure she'd gotten it! She'd won the prize!

She had been on the chemotherapy 5FU treatment only a few days so it was hard to believe the treatment had worked so well or so fast. Yet, here she was talking to me with no touch of fatigue or pain coming through. She sounded very healthy and her old self and the joyous sound of singing rang through her voice.

Doctor Elisabeth Kübler-Ross would have explained it as my mother's bargaining measures to postpone death. In her book *On Death and Dying* Dr. Kübler-Ross lists three ingredients found in bargaining.

1. It includes a prize offered "for good behavior."
2. It sets a self-imposed deadline.
3. It includes an implicit promise that the patient will not ask for more if this one postponement is granted.

In the case of a strong Christian like my mother, she had definitely bargained with the Lord using these three rules.

1. She had reminded Him that she'd served Him her whole life and she promised now that if He healed her she would resume teaching her Bible classes and be even more a testimony to God's glory.

2. She was about to turn fifty-seven and she asked for just fifteen more years—"after all, hadn't God promised us seventy years?"

3. Then she promised she would die willingly in fifteen years and not ask for a moment more. "By then your sister and brother will be married," she said to me.

She had, with great faith, marched lovingly into God's presence and struck her bargain for fifteen more years.

We phoned each other all during the month of January and she sounded stronger with every call.

The first week of February rained into California that year and with it came my mother's birthday and mine.

Her birthday card to me had her special handwritten message.

My dearest,

My every prayer and wish in a daughter has been met—in you. I ask for nothing more but that you continue in life with spiritual success, health, joy and peace.

What a joy to belong to Him and each other. I'm so thankful for the blessed fellowship we have with one another.

And just think—praise be to our Loving Saviour—we are both well and enjoying our birthdays!

Love,

MOTHER

Toward the end of that week I was taken to a friend's house and surprised by a gathering of women and a birthday luncheon.

As I came in the door of Ruth's home, I saw not only several close friends, but their mothers as well. Out of the corner of my eye, and to the right of me, I thought I saw my mother. I turned, looked directly into the living room, and did indeed see my radiant, perfectly healthy-looking mother standing there. She was the picture of health.

The last time I'd seen her was on Christmas Day when she was weak, lifeless, and her skin was cancer-colored gray.

There she stood, arms outstretched, waiting to welcome me. She had on a navy blue knit suit trimmed in red and white. Her hair had just been done, her eyes were sparkling, and her skin was lineless and a creamy, healthy beige. She was so beautiful. I stumbled over to her, hugged and kissed her, and could not believe my eyes. It was unreal.

The next day she wrote me a note. It said:

My dear Ones,

Praise God for the beautiful day that met my eyes when I awakened at 9:00 A.M. today.

I enjoyed yesterday so very much. I love my gifts—I'm going to wear and enjoy each one.

Her letter went on as she told me of some family pictures she was sending and that my sister, Marilyn, was listening to *The Sound of Music* album. Then she closed the letter by saying:

I must close and get the roast in the oven. Next Monday I go to U.C.L.A. Medical Center again—quite a routine! But thank God, I'm feeling so *very* good. On Wednesday I'm going to prayer meeting and give my testimony of healing and I'll praise God for *all* of it.

Did you know—Christ in you—that means *life?*—and I have Him and by His life—I have life!

Lovingly,
MOTHER

I saw her a day later and again I was stunned by her healing. I thought, "She's actually struck that bargain with God!" It looked for all the world as if cancer had been completely defeated.

The next day I got this note:

My dearest Joy,

How was your day on Sunday? I pray it has been a success and a blessing.

I was at U.C.L.A. today. Things are still the same. Praise God! I'm feeling great. I'm even anxious to get out and go shopping a little. [Shopping was her favorite indoor sport.]

A famous doctor was lecturing at U.C.L.A. Medical Center to several doctors. I was asked if I'd be willing to let them see and examine me. They said my case is remarkable and of course I think so too. Oh, I'm so grateful and thankful to my loving Saviour.

It's 11:00 P.M. and my bedtime. I'll say goodnite. Kisses to my children and Rickie and Laurie.

Love always,
MOTHER

Later that week, when I saw her, she was still bubbling and vivacious. She had just returned from UCLA and had been on display for some world-famous cancer specialists. The main doctor had discussed at great length her remarkable improvement. Much of the talk was too medically scientific for her to understand, but at the end of the session they showed her their chart on her. At the bottom it said, "Dramatic recovery."

We talked that day for a long time about what had happened in the past weeks. Again she told me about Christmas, when she was so ill, and how she had asked God to heal her. At the same time, many Christian friends had been seeing her or phoning and telling her she *should be well*. Over and over in those weeks she heard that:

"God can heal cancer."

"You should go to a healing service and ask So-and-So to pray for you."

"You should stop eating meat and go on a grapefruit diet."

"You should go to Mexico and get the famous cancer-cure treatment."

One lady said, "Mayo Clinic has a secret cure for breast cancer." She would pay my mother's way there. (On that one I phoned Dr. Ralph Bryon away from his strenuous duties as a surgeon at City of Hope Hospital and asked if that were true. He answered, "If it *was* true it would be no secret and not only Mayo but UCLA and every other cancer clinic in the world would have it available to their patients.")

Many Christians, in great love, unknowingly rocked my mother's world severely. Some said such thoughtless things. One woman (like one of Job's friends) kept pounding at my mother to "confess her sin." "Marion," she said on the phone one day, "come on, you can tell me—what sin are you committing?"

I wish I'd known at that moment that Mathew Henry had written of dreadful diseases as "spiritual promotions." He said:

Extraordinary afflictions are not always the punishment of extraordinary sins, but sometimes the trial of extraordinary graces. Sanctified afflictions are spiritual promotions.

I also *now* know my mother wasn't the first or the last who was put under superpressure by questions such as, "Which sin have you committed?" or, "Where *is* your faith?" Many people have been degraded and deeply hurt in this manner. And it is with deep sorrow I have to report that people *without* God rarely ask these questions. Usually Christians ask them of other Christians.

The young mother who shared her experience with me about her fifteen-year-old son's death by cancer had her experiences with

Christians, too. She told me that very early in her son's treatment she had prayed for the boy's healing. She pleaded and bargained with God to heal her son of cancer. She did not recall the exact words of the Lord, but when God did answer it had boiled down to a simple *no*. It was a quiet, almost peaceful prayer time for the mother, but the answer had been definitely, *No—he will die.*

From that moment on (in what I consider remarkable maturity) she changed the focal points of her prayers. She prayed:

1. For her son to have more pain-free moments.
2. For her son's good relationship with Christ to get even better.
3. For her son's witness at the hospital with doctors, nurses, and staff, and at home, with his brothers and sisters.

Beautifully, she began to see God immediately begin to answer *these* prayers with large *yeses*. She said her own peace of mind was incredible. She had achieved the very difficult status of accepting her son's death without a trace of morbidity or bitterness. She and her husband and family were doing just fine—just fine, that is, until word got around in their church that they were not praying for their son's complete healing of cancer.

Slowly at first, and then faster, came the criticism. She was accused of not trusting God—of doubting that God *could* heal, and worst of all—that she had a shocking lack of faith.

She was mentally and spiritually bewildered by their reactions. Daily God was doing incredibly beautiful things *through* her son's cancer. God had plainly told her of her son's approaching death, yet to accept *that* answer seemed to make her a traitor, guilty of spiritual treason.

The whole thing came to a dreadful boiling point when several pastors and deacons gathered at her home to pray for her son's complete healing. Tearfully she explained that, in her son's case, he *was terminal.* She wanted them to pray for the last months of his life. Her son was a radiant Christian teen-ager. He had accepted his serious disease and anticipated dying and being with Jesus with dignity and great joy. God had done miracles in the lives of all those who stood by his bed. She begged the ministers to pray in these directions.

I get angry every time I think about the response of these sincere men of God. They were disgusted with her lack of faith and ashamed of her for not believing God could heal cancer, and they abruptly left her home. What really dug itself into the innermost part of my soul was her next sentence. She said, "You know, Joyce, for the many months of my son's illness and until the time of his death, not one of those ministers ever came to my house or the hospital again."

We Christians can be so sure about the pieces of God's plans—so sure about God's ways—and so sure about God's mind—that we miss *entirely* His *real*, bona fide miracles cracking and popping like bright bolts of lightning all around us.

When Jesus walked this earth, He healed many, many people—He even healed Lazarus from death, but what of the thousands He did *not* heal? Was that because of their sins—so He did not heal them to punish them? No—God *does* allow suffering, but He does not sit on His high throne and hold us like little voodoo dolls in His hand and poke pins and needles into us to punish us for our sins.

When the pastors told the mother to pray for her son's healing and she said no, they tried, convicted, and sentenced her for not accepting God's healing.

It was Joe Bayly who wrote, in *The View From a Hearse*, "Death for the Christian should be a shout of triumph, through sorrow and tears, bringing glory to God—not a confused misunderstanding of the will of God to heal."

Not long ago a lady, twice widowed, shared with me her experience of bargaining with God about healing the life of her husband.

She had lost her first husband after thirty years of marriage. Two years later she had married again and had seven happy years with a second husband. Then he got cancer.

She told me they had been so very happy and the seven years had been so short that she pleaded and bargained with God to heal her husband. He was very close to dying and she knelt by his bed and begged the Lord to heal him so he wouldn't die. She said the Lord's voice spoke so clearly she was quite startled by it. She heard Him say very distinctly in her mind, *Your husband has prepared himself to accept death and to die right now. Tell Me, do you*

want him to prepare himself for death again—later on? She opened
her eyes and looked at her husband—he was at peace—he had
reached acceptance. She said, "Oh, Joyce, I knew right then I'd
have to release him. I didn't want to make him go through that
again—later on—so I released him. At that moment a great peace
settled over me. He died a few hours later. *Both* of us were at
peace."

If she had hung on, begged God to let her husband live, she
would have missed what God wanted to do in their lives. Instead,
she released her husband into the arms of God and began being the
widow God wanted her to be. She was grateful for those marvelous
seven years, sad that he was gone, but alive and excited about living
today's day out.

She was a very different widow from the one I read about in
Charles L. Allen's book *When You Lose a Loved One*. He told of
a woman whose husband was dying. In fact, the doctor had said
he was gone. The children became hysterical and begged their
mother to pray. So she knelt down, prayed, and asked God to bring
her husband back to life. The man opened his eyes, recovered,
and lived nine more years. Of those nine years, Mr. Allen wrote,
"But those nine years were for him so painful and unhappy that no
less than a thousand times did she [the wife] regret that God
answered her prayer."

It's funny how we love to talk about Jesus raising Lazarus, but
what we never seem to consider is that at a later date Lazarus
died. He did not live forever. We don't know how many years his
miraculous stay of death lasted, but we can know for certain he
did die. I wonder how his health was during those years, but I
particularly wonder what Martha's and Mary's thoughts were when
he died a *second time.*

In my mother's case—when she was so ill at Christmas—she was
very pressured by Christians about healing. It was almost as if she
had to have a miraculous healing. It seemed she had to have a healing to *prove* that her love, faith, and trust in God was alive and
well. She especially had to prove it to a lady in the church who
insisted she *must* be sinning. "No one gets cancer, my dear," she
snidely mentioned to Mother, "unless there is sin in their life!"

Actually we catch cancer and death and dying because we all

have been exposed to the germs of sin produced way back by Adam and Eve. We all have sinned—and ever since that fateful day in the Garden of Eden we have been experiencing the diseases of life and steadily we have been dying from them.

I also want to state right here and now that before my mother's illness, during it, and right this moment, I believe with all my heart in divine healing. It does not boggle my mind that God can heal any illness. A God who made us in the first place can most certainly heal all our diseases.

During my mother's illness, though, I restricted God to only one kind of healing. I now know God heals in many, many ways and is not narrowly limited by one method only. I have listed here only four of His ways. But in the time of Mother's illness I thought the only healing was:

1. *Spontaneously!*

On at least three occasions in my childhood, my parents prayed over me during a desperate illness. Instantly and spontaneously, I was well. Many other times when the illness was not too serious they would pray over the fever only to have it drop, and by the next day I would be completely recovered. Other people have gone to healing services and God has instantly healed them.

So I am long acquainted with God's instant healings, but when I talked with my mother in January about her miraculous healing, something never clicked about it. I grew uneasy when she repeated, "God has completely *cured* me." For some reason the last three words of that were difficult to swallow and they stuck in my throat like a small, irritating fish bone. I felt guilty immediately about this because it seemed to indicate a lack of faith on my part. Why couldn't I accept the word "cured"? Why wasn't I ecstatic with joy and thanksgiving? Didn't I believe God could heal?

I drove home from visiting Mother one day late in February in the slow lane of the freeway. It took almost an extra hour to get home, but I needed time to sort out what I'd seen and heard. My thoughts and emotions were very mixed up.

"Obviously," I thought, "she looks, acts and feels *cured*. I can't argue with that kind of visual success. I know God has healed her spontaneously, but—" and for the first time a new thought about healing rose up in my mind—"what if she has not been cured, but only given a remission, a stay of execution, or a reprieve? Is that healing of a sort, too?"

I changed lanes, to the fastest lane in the center, and shoved the accelerator down hard for the last miles before my turnoff.

February rained itself into March that year, but my mother walked in nothing but pure sunshine. Her health was never better. April found us happily shopping occasionally and my mother's Bible classes were filled to overflow crowds with women eager to learn. Many women, long estranged from God, found their way into her classes and with the sensitive and warm introduction that was only hers, they met her friend—her Lord and Saviour, Jesus.

The twelfth of May brought Mother's Day around and she sent a card to me. It was signed (never by just "Mother"), "From a loving mother who is proud and grateful for such a precious daughter."

I flipped the card over and read on the back page:

My dearest Joyce,

I didn't think at one time back a few months ago that I would live to enjoy Mother's Day with my loved ones.

But here I am—better and stronger—and in no pain *whatever!* Praise God!

I shall never cease to praise Him for His touch on my body and the marvelous miracle of healing performed.

My prayer is that I may be worthy of His love and serve Him with joy with my new health and strength.

And I thank Him for my dear, dear children. May He bless and keep you all.

Always with love,

MOTHER

I thought, "Well, that's that. She was right. She *is* cured. I was wrong to have doubts. She has experienced the *spontaneous* healing. She has bargained with God and has received her extended fifteen years."

Psalm 116 became my mother's source of proof. I'm not sure, but she may even have memorized it. Obviously, David had experienced the bargaining stage because he described it very aptly.

Death stared me in the face—I was frightened and sad. Then I cried, "Lord, save me!" How kind he is! How good he is! So merciful, this God of ours! The Lord protects the simple and the childlike; I was facing death and then he saved me. Now I can relax. For the Lord has done this wonderful miracle for me. He has saved me from death, my eyes from tears, my feet from stumbling. I shall live! Yes, in his presence—here on earth!

In my discouragement I thought, "They are lying when they say I will recover." But now what can I offer Jehovah for all he has done for me? I will bring him an offering of wine and praise his name for saving me. I will publicly bring him the sacrifice I vowed I would. His loved ones are very precious to him and he does not lightly let them die.

Psalms 116:3–15

My mother was also very familiar with a man named Hezekiah in the Book of Isaiah. Since she taught Old Testament, and knew it like the back of her hand, she had used this passage in her bargaining with God.

She knew very well that Hezekiah was told by the Lord, "Set your affairs in order, for you are going to die; you will not recover from this illness" (Isaiah 38:1).

She knew that when he got this news bulletin he turned his face to the wall and bargained like mad with God. He reminded God of how he'd served and obeyed Him and then he just "broke down with great sobs" (Isaiah 38:3).

Mother also knew Hezekiah had been heard by God and was given years more to live. (Right! Fifteen years, to be exact.)

She rationalized her breast surgery and illness exactly as Hezekiah had when he wrote a poem about his illness. Among other things, he said:

Yes, now I see it all—it was good for me to undergo this bitterness, for you have lovingly delivered me from death; you have forgiven all my sins. For dead men cannot praise you. They cannot be filled with hope and joy. The living, only the living, can praise you as I do today. . . . Think of it! The Lord healed me!

Isaiah 38:17–20

My mother recounted Hezekiah's experience and rejoiced that it was her experience, too. She had fifteen more years.

But my doubts would not lie down and be quiet. There was never a more confusing time in my life as in those months with my mother while I tried to sort out my emotions and feelings regarding healing.

Actually, my passing thought that God might have other ways of healing was the key, but it was a long time later when the Lord sorted it out for me. I was to find out God heals not only spontaneously, but:

2. *Gradually.*

I remembered the time immediately after a surgery of mine. I'd had the finest of doctors, several specialists were consulted. I had top nursing care, great intensive care, and all was geared to meet my recovery needs.

But it was very apparent that after the doctors had done their best work, after the surgery tools were sterilized and put away, everyone had to wait. Nothing more could be done. We all had to wait for God's gradual healing to take place.

I talked to Dr. Jim White about this *gradual* type healing of God. He told me of praying before each and every surgery and how he asked the Lord for all the skill and wisdom his training had given him to be put into use. "However," he said, "I learned early in my practice that as a surgeon I could relieve and heal *pain* in my patients but only God could heal *suffering.* After I've done my best work, I always have to stand back and watch as only God can heal the body and the mind and make recovery possible."

I asked him if he had ever heard a patient bargaining for more time. He smiled and said, "No, not directly, but once I *definitely* bargained with God over a patient."

Then he told me how he had prayed as usual before surgery, operated, and felt all was progressing routinely well. Three days after the operation, the man's progress reversed itself and he started to deteriorate. Dr. White and the entire staff couldn't find any rhyme or reason for it. The man's condition continued downward and, finally, thirty days after a routine surgery, the patient was comatose and obviously dying. Dr. White said, "Then I went before the Lord and asked God to give this man's life back to him. I told the Lord I would level with the family and give God all the honor if He would spare this man's life." Almost overnight, the man recovered. Dr. White went to the family and said, "As a doctor I did everything I could possibly do and he was dying in spite of all our work. I asked God to raise him up and God answered my prayer. I'm telling you this because I promised God I'd give Him the honor—it was His doing—God's miracle—not mine." It was another time when God granted a *gradual* healing.

God also heals:

3. *Circumstantially.*

That's exactly the type healing that had taken place in the lives of the mother and her dying teen-age son. God did not heal the son or take away the bone cancer, but He healed people and circumstances all around it. He healed the mother's and father's anxious hearts. He healed the grieving hearts of the brothers and sisters. And during the boy's hospital stay God healed doctors, nurses, technicians, and many staff people.

My millionaire friend Mary Korstjens, the beautiful lady I wrote about in *The Richest Lady in Town,* is the recipient of circumstantial healing. God has not healed her of polio or taken away her from-the-neck-down paralysis, but He has brought *circumstantial* healing to Mary, her husband, her family, and to scores of people around her. Every once in a while a group of Christians will—with great faith and sincerity—pray for her healing from paralysis. They miss the important fact that she has *already* been healed. God's plan did not include removal of the basic problem (polio), but rather He chose to heal the circumstances around her.

Von Letherer, my friend and agent, to whom this book is dedicated, has just been returned to the hospital for treatments. Yesterday I talked with his wife, Joanne, and she said, "Of course we have always wanted God to completely heal Von of his disease—but I wonder—if God had healed Von years ago and made him well— wouldn't we have missed all the miracles God wanted to share *through* this painful illness? I think so and I also think Von is the special man of God he is because he has allowed God to lead him through his whole life of thirty-seven years of pain and sickness."

Von and Joanne are living their lives within the framework of circumstantial healing.

There is a fourth way God heals:

4. *Temporarily.*

It is the type of healing medical science calls a remission. Some remissions are incredible. In leukemia, patients experiencing a remission can live with all the symptoms of the disease practically nonexistent. They can last weeks, months, or even years. The disease seems to stop all its activity or growth and the patient resumes a nearly normal life.

I was familiar with this word (*remission*) during my mother's illness, but I did not think of it consciously as being a healing from God. Subconsciously, though, it was beginning to really take shape. I felt a little guilty for not trusting God for a *cure*.

I was beginning to think, just barely, about the word *remission*. So one day I asked Mother if she thought God had cured her or was she in a medical remission? She went completely out of character, for her, and grew cold and distant. She said, distinctly, "No remission—God's *cured* me. You'll see."

I felt something like a cactus needle pricking the back of my mind. I felt it later when my dad handed her a gift. It was a beautiful, leather, lady's attaché case. She held it up and said, "Oh, look at this. It's for my notebooks to take to my Bible-study classes. I'm going to need this for teaching now that I am well." The needle bit into my flesh again.

She continued to amaze everyone (including me) with great health all during the next few months.

The sixth month of that year—June—came and the warm color of her skin changed ever so slightly into a grayed beige. I noticed, but brushed it out of my mind.

June, as it sometimes is in California, was cool, but around the end of it and into the first week of July the weather blistered out into its finest dry heat.

On the Fourth of July our whole family gathered at my parents' home. Their new swimming pool was full of splashing water and noisy cousins and relatives.

In the midst of all the helloing and hugging and kissing going on, I got a quick look at my mother's face.

Instantly the cactus punched thousands of holes in my mind because I knew she had not been cured—but given a remission. She had asked for fifteen years more. She had thought she had it. She had not heard the Lord clearly for He had answered her request by saying, *No, Marion, not fifteen years—only six months.*

I can look back on that scene by the pool now and see that she did not have a *spontaneous, gradual,* or *circumstantial* healing, but a *temporary* healing. It was a beautiful temporary healing which added six months of pain-free time to her life—six months when she served God with a higher amount of devotion and love than anybody had within a thousand-mile radius. I will always praise God for giving her those six months of freedom from pain. It doesn't even matter that I did not understand what type of healing was done or that I was confused by it all. I'm just grateful to God for those months.

Mother did not have to tell me new lumps had formed, like globules of cement on her remaining breast—I just knew. She didn't have to tell me that the pains in her chest were beginning to be unbearable. I could see.

I sat on the edge of the pool that Fourth of July trying to keep my heart under control. I faked light, small-talk conversation with everyone and, all in all, you could have said we had a wonderful family holiday—except for the brief moments when someone wasn't talking to me and I idly kicked and stirred circles in the water. It was then I wondered what I would do the first time some well-meaning Christian lady said to me, "What do you mean, 'Marion is dying'? Why, God healed her. *Marion* said so!" What would I answer her? I didn't even have any answers for me—much less for anyone else.

My mother called me out of my thoughts to come and eat something. I left the pool, sat down with everyone, and found the food (no matter how hard I tried) would not go past my tongue.

I felt like I had accidently fallen into a deep, dark, hidden pit. It was the pit of grief, and as I fell I tried to catch something, anything, to break the fall. But my fingers frantically clawed the sides and nothing stopped my rapid descent. I fell and fell and fell, and kept on endlessly falling for days and days and days.

Mother had bargained with God and He had given her a temporary remission, but it was over.

In music there is a term which fits my mother's bargaining with

God for added life to a fine tee: *rubato*. According to my dictionary, *rubato* means, "robbing or taking from the notes their strict time value by alternately hurrying and retarding for the purpose of expression."

The *rubato*ed notes of the song of bargaining had ended for my mother. The six months were used up—no more could be accomplished—and so she began her serious dying.

6

Regardless and Always

Her sun is gone down while it is yet
day.

JEREMIAH 15:9

There were brief moments during that raging-hot July when I
stopped falling in the pit of grief and depression, but not many.

In the middle of that month, I called Mother to ask if she wanted
to go shopping. She sounded tired and very ill, but her voice
brightened upon hearing the word *shopping* and she said she'd
love to go.

I picked her up and drove her to Topanga Plaza shopping center.
We were both doing what we loved to do. (My mother was like my
friend, Carolyn, who—according to her husband—has committed
to memory entire floor plans of every department store in the area.)

We were silly and full of fun that day in Ohrbach's as we walked
from one department to another. I forgot about falling into pits.

We laughed at some loosely crocheted bikini bathing suits—they had large holes in them and were *un*lined if you can picture that. In the hat department I tried on a large, floppy hat, struck what I hoped was a "movie star pose," and said, "Ta-Da!" My mother responded instantly with, "Oh, Julie Andrews, may I have your autograph?" Several clerks grew suspicious of us and that made it all the more fun.

After we'd examined everything on the first and second floors, we came back down the escalator and went into the boys' department. Mother bought our son, Rick, a shirt and as we waited at the cashier stand she said, "It's funny, but my memory seems to be getting worse. I know Rickie's birthday is coming up on August the ninth, but I'm worried that I'll forget. You take this shirt home and give it to him. Okay?" She got her change and package and we resumed shopping. She bought both my sister, Marilyn, and our daughter, Laurie, a pair of sandals.

While we were looking at some blouses, I realized Mother had slowed her walking pace down and had grown quiet. I looked at my watch and discovered we'd been there almost two hours. I suggested that we go home, but she said no, and protested she was fine. About then I remembered a pair of slippers I'd wanted to check out so I told her to wait at the blouse counter and I'd be right back. I hurried down the aisle and found the slippers.

Just as the clerk asked me if I wanted any help, something made me look back down the aisle at Mother. The store was rather crowded with people, but for that instant I had a clear look down the aisle at my mother's head and shoulder profile. She was just standing there looking downward and was very pale.

The clerk said, "Are these the size you were looking for?" I may have answered her out loud, but I think not. All I do remember is that I put the slippers back into her hands.

"My mother is dying. We will never come to this place again. She is standing there saying good-bye to this store—her old friend. My God, help me to be strong." I pushed as fast as I could through the crowds toward her.

I slipped one arm around her and, with my free hand, took her packages. She was having a hard time breathing.

"Let's go home, Mother," I said. She didn't move. I knew she

wanted one more moment to say good-bye so I just waited. In a
minute or so I said, "We must go now." With her quiet, "all right,"
we moved slowly toward the parking-lot entrance.

There were perhaps four hundred or so people in the store that
day, but I'm sure none of them knew of the personal drama taking
place. I left her at the entrance on the sidewalk, ran to the car, and
drove back to pick her up. I'm sure no one paid any attention to
the tired, worn-looking lady in the blue dress. No one saw her turn,
look back into the store and, ever so slightly, nod farewell. She got
into the car, settled herself, and (pretending I was her chauffeur)
gave a little smile and said, "Home, James!"

It was a memorable day for both of us. It was a day of my knowing she was dying and of her knowing that not only she was dying,
but that we and all she loved would die to her.

Within my head I heard grief's song transpose from a major key
down into the sad lament of a minor key. It was a strange sound,
haunting and even beautiful, in its own way—but oh, so disturbing
and to hear it was to cry softly.

Our sense of loss, loneliness, and grief was overwhelming. Both
Mother and I knew tremendous depression that day. Hers was in a
different direction from mine, but both of us were suffering from
what Dr. Kübler-Ross calls "reactive depression." Later I saw my
mother go into the other type of depression Dr. Ross calls "pre-
paratory" and it was beautiful to watch her move through its dark
tunnel and out the other side to acceptance.

The next day after that shopping trip, and during my prayer time,
I came to the main issue in my life at that moment—coping with
(incredible thought) my mother's real, about-to-happen death. I
had a full schedule of singing and speaking. At that time I had my
own daily fifteen-minute radio show. Being a wife and mother to my
husband and children was the top priority on my list of goals. So the
schedule I was keeping wound me tight around its finger.

"Lord," I prayed, "*when* she dies—as I now know she will—tell me
in advance when death is near. I want to spend her last weeks with
her. I'll cancel all engagements, prerecord my radio program, freeze
extra casseroles for my family, and do everything so I can be with
her. I do not want to let my own hesitancy about dying keep me
from facing it or from being with her.

"Please, Lord, I want no regrets after she's gone. I don't want to think I was so busy with my little world I didn't take time to wait with her while she died. So Lord, please tell me *when*."

My friend Marilu told me that when she was notified of her nine-and-one-half-year-old son's death after his second surgery, her very first thought was, "Oh, I didn't give him a birthday party on his ninth birthday." Fortunately, she worked through her natural, mother-type regrets.

But I remember an old man at Los Angeles International Airport who broke my heart over his regrets. We were both waiting to board a jet to Hawaii. I was on my way overseas to do a speaking-and-singing tour for the United States Army Chaplains. The man was just sitting beside me when, out of the corner of my eye, I noticed he was very silently sitting there crying. I was about to ask him if I could help when a man on the other side of him did it for me.

The old man just shook his head *no* and continued to cry. When he got a firmer grip on himself, he began talking—not to anyone in particular, but out loud as to why he was on his way to Hawaii. He told about his wife nagging him for thirty years about taking a Hawaiian vacation. Twenty years ago, when they had become financially able to afford such a trip, she really nagged him. He had firmly said *no* and given her his reasons. After all, Hawaii held no interest for him and he couldn't see any point in going all that way and paying all that money to see an island or two.

Then he said, "Six months ago she got cancer and now—now, she's gone." His tears were streaming down his face, but he made no move to dry them. He just continued, "Before she died, she made me promise I'd go and take that vacation in Hawaii for her— so here I am alone—going to Hawaii. God, why didn't I take her when we had all that time and all those years?"

I sat very still for a long time, thinking about the things I should do in my own life so I'd have no such sad trips to make.

I studied the old man because while he did have a grievous regret, he *was* definitely working through it by keeping a promise made to his dying wife and I loved him for it!

At anyone's death there are bound to be some regrets, but I'd hoped that in my mother's case I wouldn't have any or at least they'd be held at a minimum. I prayed the regrets I might experience would not become a detriment to my own healing after her death.

My unedited notes, taken at that time, were dated, "Last week of July," and I'd scribbled:

8:30 A.M.

I've tried not to think of her today—but it's hard not to. Even as I read the newspaper this morning something kept vaguely disturbing my reading. It was a dull, rather ordinary pain, but very persistent.

When I finished the (already) depressing newspaper, the pain got sharper. Then I remembered—

Today, Mother goes to U.C.L.A. Medical Center. This time for the isotope (or something like that) treatments.

Yesterday, when I phoned her, her voice sounded so weak. I asked her if she was in any pain. She answered, "Oh, yes, the swelling in my chest is up. The fluid needs to be drained again. You might say this is a very bad day physically—but (her tone brightened with the rest of the sentence) spiritually and mentally I couldn't be better!"

While it wasn't in my notes, I remember in that same phone conversation she especially emphasized that I not bother going to the hospital to see her. She said the doctors had told her she would receive the chemotherapy, inhalation treatments, and be home by the weekend in three days.

I decided not to make the trip to visit her during that brief stay, called a florist, and ordered a bouquet of flowers to be delivered to her room.

The day she went in, I was neck-deep in all kinds of activities—prearranged schedules, etc.—but by late afternoon I changed my mind and I knew I had to go see her.

Dick got home from work and I said, "I don't know why, but can we go to UCLA and see Mother?"

After dinner we drove the hour or so across Los Angeles to the hospital.

The University of California's Los Angeles Medical Center looks as picture perfect as any other large, active, busily engaged hospital.

We had to go through the emergency entrance where the busy business of living and dying was taking place. The halls painted hospital green, the medicinal smells of Lysol, Clorox, and rubbing alcohol hit me as two of the reasons why I am not entirely at ease in hospitals. However, in that area of the hospital it wasn't so much the walls and aroma that got to me, but rather the people.

Doctors were talking together in tight little circles, looking too young to be making so many responsible life-and-death decisions. Nurses stood or sat writing out their endless reports, registering either boredom or fatigue on their faces. Technicians sauntered down the halls with trays of blood-test samples as casually as if they were carrying tubes of tomato juice. The cleaning staff was valiantly trying to work their floor-wash equipment in and around gurneys, clustered doctors, patients, and distraught families.

As we neared the elevator a little girl, being carried by her mother, vomited over her mother's shoulder and it splashed onto the clean, shiny floor. A cleaning man behind me muttered a sigh and said, "That's the third time I've done that floor today," and moved his pail back toward the mess.

We pushed the third-floor button and the elevator's quiet motor noise came as a few seconds of welcome relief.

The moment we stepped off the elevator onto the third floor, we had no trouble finding my mother's room—even though it was down at the end of a long corridor. It took the grand prize for noise! I was guided down the hall by my mother's laughter.

"It was dumb to make this long trip over here for nothing," I thought. She sounded absolutely fine.

She was the only person I saw when I entered the room. Sitting cross-legged on the middle of her bed, she was reading aloud some cards and letters she'd received. There she sat, in a darling robe, looking fresh as a daisy. She let out a whoop of joy when she saw us and said, "What in the world are you two doing here?" For the second time in two minutes, I wondered that myself. She looked marvelous.

We said hello to my dad and were introduced to Mother's roommate in the bed across the room. It was right after that I came and stood at the foot of Mother's bed. She was showing me the bouquet which had been delivered from me and she was thanking us. I stood there looking at what was the poorest excuse for an expensive florist arrangement I'd ever seen and was thinking, "Next time I'll send candy." Mother thought the flowers were just lovely and was saying so when I heard it the first time. A voice clearly said, *She is dying now.*

My mother thought my outburst of, "Ha!" was in response to her statements about the flowers, but actually I couldn't believe the words I'd heard. I was not able to fit their message with the visual picture of my mother.

I took one giant step backward into denial and told myself she might die, but certainly it would not be now.

Then I heard it again. *She is dying now.* I wondered if anyone else had heard it.

A few minutes later, I pulled my father aside and said, "Dad, have the doctors said anything to you about Mother's condition?"

"Oh, yes," he said cheerfully. "They think she's doing just great. They say she'll be home in two days."

Just then two doctors came in. They were eager to say hello to Mother and loudly they renewed their previously established friendship with her.

She is dying. Now. The third time I heard it, I said in my heart, "Lord—look at her. Look at the doctors, look at my father. *They* think she's fine. Am I the only one who knows?"

You asked Me to tell you when she would die. I am telling you—now. The quiet answer was loud enough for me to hear even above the noisy din of Mother's room.

I followed the doctors out into the hall. "Doctor," I called to one of them, "I'm Mrs. Miller's daughter. I'm a big girl and have had my share of tragic blows. I do not want to be coddled or spared anything relative to my mother's condition. So please tell me what the prognosis is." Both doctors looked at me and then at each other in amazement. "Why, she's just fine. This is a routine trip for her. Now, don't you worry. She'll be out of here by Friday."

"No, I don't think so," I said to myself and walked back to Mother's room.

While I was gone the inhalation therapist had set up her equipment and had begun Mother's treatment.

I was still thinking about the words the Lord had so clearly spoken. My mother mistook my worried look. She took off her oxygen mask and said, "Oh, honey—don't let this bother you—it just helps me breathe and after I've had this treatment I feel so much better."

We stayed for a little longer, then said our good-byes and started down the hall toward the elevators. The green hall began to spin and swirl around me so I reached for the railing mounted on the wall. Dick's arm went around me instead.

"Honey," he said, "I think you better prepare yourself. I don't think your mother is ever going to leave here alive."

His words restored my sanity. "Thank the Lord you know, too. I thought I was the only one who knew she's dying." I started crying on the elevator and didn't stop for three days.

The next day I received a long letter from Mother. She had written it an hour before she'd gone to UCLA. It was the very last letter she was to write.

Evidently, on the day she was to go to UCLA, she'd felt better than she had in a long time so she backtracked from acceptance down into the bargaining stage. At one point in her letter she wrote:

Today I go to U.C.L.A. again. I'm sure of the promise and love of God and know He will completely heal me. He said it was finished and by His stripes I am healed. He promises seventy years and by reason of strength even eighty—I think I, as a Christian who has the *life of Christ* within her, can claim health.

I do not ask in my merits—but as a child of God redeemed—I ask in Jesus' name! God does not heal because I deserve it—but because Jesus paid for it and redeemed *me*. Praise God.

I wished I could believe that God would heal her. I wished I had her confidence—but I simply didn't. However, the last lines at the end of her letter told me that God was preparing her, not for healing—but for death—in spite of what she'd written about healing.

She had written the letter in her typical breezy style and her handwriting reflected a bit of hurry. Then, just before her signature at the bottom of the page, she must have stopped, even if briefly, because written very clearly, deliberately, and legibly was her last, but most important message to me. She wrote clearly—so I'd not miss it:

It's almost noon, I must close and get ready to go at 1:00 P.M. So much love and prayer to you all my dear children.

Keep faith with God—*regardless and always.*

Lovingly your

MOTHER

Also one of your ardent fans!

MOM

My eyes went back to the one-liner about keeping faith with God —regardless and always. This was her written farewell. *Regardless* —of what would or might or could happen—*and always,* forever, until we'd meet again were the words of the legacy she left.

She didn't come home on that weekend and nobody but me seemed upset. The doctors just smiled and assured us that she would stay over the weekend, but would *certainly* be home by Wednesday.

But when Wednesday rolled around, everyone at the hospital got very quiet and they never set a release date again.

She had been in the hospital less than a week by the time I checked my schedules, cancelled engagements, and made my family comfortable so I could be there.

I was shocked at what I saw when I walked into her room. In those brief days she had gone from bright-eyed and bushy-tailed enthusiasm to flat-on-her-back breathing with an oxygen mask.

Denial had stamped itself into anger. Anger had burned out into bargaining. Bargaining dissipated itself into depression and grief. Finally, grief began to lift into tired, quiet acceptance. The dying had begun.

It was then as I visited her that day she asked me to help her sit up. So I cranked the bed up and she took off the oxygen mask and laid it beside her. That was the moment she *told* me about teaching me how a Christian lives for my thirty-four years and that now she was going to show me how a Christian dies. Typically of her, she was dramatic, spiritual, and completely practical because immediately after her poignantly beautiful words, she reached over to her nightstand, slid open a drawer, and brought out a yellow legal pad of paper.

Handing me the pad and a new ball-point pen, she said, "Here, take notes."

"You're kidding," I thought. "You want me to take notes of my own mother's dying? *Impossible!*"

I looked down at the pad and saw the words, "Book titles" at the top of the page. Under that were nine titles of what appeared to be women's books.

She watched my face as I read them and then said, "Oh, those are just some titles you might want to write a book under. I was thinking about the publisher who asked you to write and I jotted down some ideas for titles. You write the books, honey, I'll do the hard part," she laughed.

Oh, Dr. Elisabeth Kübler-Ross, you were so right when you said the dying have much to teach us. Very few of us are willing to pick up the notebook and pen to be students because tuition is too costly. Standing by, leaning on, and lying by our teacher seems an endless, bittersweet task. Poignant conversation and painful fatigue seem to blend together. They fill up every crevice and crack in us until finally it oozes out all our pores and we don't want to learn. But, oh, the lessons!

While Mother didn't know how long she'd have, she must have sensed it would be brief. Every day of the seven weeks I was with her, I felt like I was cramming for some kind of final exam.

The notebook pad was given to me for a twofold purpose. She knew me well enough to know I needed to do something creative with my time while I was waiting with her. She told me a number of times she was worried about my speaking schedule. "What have you done—*cancelled* them?" she asked in a pseudoshocked tone. When I told her I had, her mind instantly began to devise a plan to keep me busy. (Did she know about *this* book and how heavily I'd rely on those notes of mine? I wonder.) Secondly, she was thinking beyond the moment of her death. I'm sure she wanted to make certain I'd work through my grief. Wisdom told her that one of the best ways for me to do that was to physically pick up a pen and write on a project: hence, the book titles.

By writing down nine titles, she knew she'd be helping me develop the special resources I'd need in finding myself after her death. The titles were designed to force me into thinking about writing and other outlets so that my self-centered preoccupation with grief would end and I'd move into a creative direction. I think she knew enough about human nature to know that actually writing books would cost a superhuman amount of effort and concentration, but she did not want to think I'd be left sitting around in apathy, vegetating and rotting away with each new day. So she gave me a project.

Yesterday, after the funeral of Mrs. Harms—a friend of mine (and of my mother)—I walked up to the casket to say my good-byes. She looked just lovely. She was Ruth's mother and had been present at the birthday luncheon Ruth had given for my mother and me. I bent over the casket and told her I loved her hair. It was just beautiful and just the way she would have wanted it. Then I said, "For goodness sake, Mom Harms, don't forget to tell my mother I *wrote* all those books she told me to!" My mother had been so right in knowing I'd need a project.

No lesson my mother taught was more of an object lesson than the moment she gave me a familiar pink cardboard box. She had come to the hospital to stay only three days. Her little overnight bag had held some nighties, a robe, and the little pink box.

"Honey," she said one day, "take my pink box. I won't be needing it anymore." I opened the box up, intending to show her she'd be sorry if I took it home, but I shut it up and put it by my purse after I'd looked at it. Her personal items—curlers, hairbrush and comb, lipstick, powder, cleansing cream, lotion, toothpaste—all those things were being given to me to help me accept the inevitable.

She had moved into acceptance and wanted, without words, to help me move graciously into it.

"Some of those cosmetics are excellent products—expensive and very good. Use them in good health, honey!" (I really choked on that one.)

A doctor once told me he could always tell when a woman patient was getting well. She'd begin combing her hair or she'd put on a little lipstick—especially if visiting hours were about to happen. He always watched for these signs to check his patient's progress toward recovery.

With my mother, the opposite was true. When she accepted dying, she knew she'd no longer need combs, brushes, or cosmetics so she made a big deal of giving them to me.

The day after she gave them to me, a friend of ours came to

visit her. When Eleanor left, my mother asked—rather confidentially
—"How did Eleanor think I looked?" I asked her what she meant.
"Well, honey, I mean I've changed [she pointed to her face]. Did
she notice it or say anything about it?"

As a matter of fact, Eleanor had mentioned the enormous physical
changes she'd seen. The last time Eleanor had been with Mother
was at the birthday luncheon Ruth had given for Mother and me.
Mother was in the pink of condition then, but now she looked like
a dying woman of eighty years or more.

I realized, for the first time, that the dying are very aware of
the physical changes that are occurring and they are afraid if they
become ugly or disfigured they will be unlovable.

Even though she'd seen no mirror, she knew she had lost much
weight and, by now, was nothing more than tightly drawn gray
skin over bones. Her short hair hung limp and lifeless around her
face.

I said, "Mother, Eleanor knows you are very sick and she understood about your hair. It didn't bother her."

"Oh, I'm glad, I must look a mess."

To cheer her, I said, "That's right—as a matter of fact, you look
crummy—but I love every crummy thing about you." A tiny smile
played across her mouth and she hit the ball right back to me with,
"You don't look so hot yourself. Have you thought of leaving here
and going home to wash your hair?"

This was the only time we talked about appearances, but from
then on I made a special point of lightly brushing her hair and
reassuring her she looked much better after I'd used my magic
touch. Both of us knew I was at a complete loss in the hair-combing
department and we both knew our conversation was a game, but it
eased her mind and helped her to know we were not about to stop
loving her just because she was physically changing.

My notes tell me that isotope couldn't be used. "They inserted a
drainage tube today and Cliff flew home from Vietnam," I stated
cryptically.

One morning, while everyone was still generally optimistic about
my mother's condition, I thought my brother should be home. However, my dad was deep into denial and said he didn't think Mother's
illness was serious enough to send for Cliff. I remember being ter-

ribly angry with him. I decided to take matters into my own hands so I went back to the hospital and said, "Mother, you are so sick. Don't you think we ought to get Cliff out of Vietnam and home? Wouldn't you like to see him?" She opened her eyes very wide and said, "Oh, yes!" My dad meekly said *fine* and called the Red Cross. Less than eighteen hours later my brother, right out of the mine-infested jungles of Vietnam, went to see Mother. I had left the hospital to spend a couple of hours at home and had barely missed seeing him. Cliff took one look at Mother and phoned me at home. "What's going on?" he almost yelled. "How come nobody told me she was terminal? She's *dying*, Joyce." He was a marine corpsman and had dealt with the wounded and dying on Vietnam battlefields for months. Death was part of his regular daily routine. He went on to say not one of Dad's letters had even said *anything* remotely serious about Mother. Why hadn't Dad leveled with him, he wanted to know.

As I have said in an earlier chapter, I wish I'd known more about denial. I wish I'd been familiar with denial's shapes, attitudes, words, and actions. I think I could have explained it so much better to myself and my brother that day. Instead, I just told him how angry I was with Dad. So many times I'd gotten off the elevator on UCLA's third floor, started toward the left corridor, and I'd hear someone whistling, humming, or singing, and happily jingle-jangling his keys—I knew it would be my father. The meeting and conversation there by the nurses' station would always be the same.

"Hi, sweetie—" he'd say so cheerfully.

"Hi, Dad—how's Mother right now?" Then every bone in my body would tense and scream in unison—*please, please* don't tell me, "She's *just fine*."

"Why, she's just fine," he'd answer.

One day I could hold it in no longer. "Dad—how can you say that? She's lost weight, she's not able to sit up anymore. She's on oxygen all the time. Her skin is gray. She's dying and she knows it!"

"Oh, now Joyce." He put his arms around my stiffening shoulders, patted me, and said, "Why, all she needs is some of Grandma Uzon's Hungarian chicken soup."

"Terrific," I thought. "What all these brilliant doctors heading up cancer-research teams don't know is that Hungarian chicken soup is the answer!"

He went off down the hall whistling and doing his thing with the keys. (I think he went to Grandma's to get some soup.)

A nurse came out of a room, recognized me, and asked, "Could I have a minute with you, Mrs. Landorf?" Then very secretively she said, "Ah—your father is a minister, right?"

"Right," I said.

"Well, that makes it even harder to understand."

"Harder to understand what?" I asked.

"Well, he's had people in his congregation die and surely he knows about terminally ill patients—ah—doesn't he know your mother is terminal?"

I explained that I had just practically screamed the news at him, but he wouldn't hear me.

By now Mother had been there almost five weeks. The doctors were more than puzzled. My notes are short, but graphic here.

Doctor C. said, "Prognosis is poor—very poor. I don't know how she can get any sicker than she is and still live."

Dad keeps on talking to us as if she has a chest cold. I don't know how I can stand the strain of his attitude. He is very mad at Cliff because Cliff told him the Lord *might* take Mother home very soon.

Dad listened to Doctor C., nodded his head like he understood the words, but walked away without hearing a thing.

Mother is now on an IV of dextrose and is being catheterized. All that's left of her is her beautiful brown eyes—cancer has taken everything else.

Two days later, my notes are supershort—"*Now* he says—all she needs is vitamins!"

Later that day, he bought the new refrigerator. "Why, Dad?" I limply asked, knowing the answer before he spoke.

"Why, our old fridge is on the fritz and when she gets home she'll love this new one."

Then, as he was going down the hall he said something about, "I'm thinking about going down to the travel agency. You know your mother always wanted to go to Hawaii—"

I came close to being terminal that instant or going stark, raving insane at that moment—but never quite knew which.

I went home for a few hours of rest only to have the worst (and to date *only*) argument with my sister, Marilyn.

She was standing in Laurie's bedroom and she looked so darling. There is twenty years difference in our ages and she's only a year and a half older than our son, Rick. I've always loved her as one of my own rather than as a sister. Our conversation started quietly enough with her question: "Will Mother get better?"

Most experts feel children should have their questions on death and sex answered in the same manner. We should be truthful, but answer only the immediate question. We should not run ahead of the child with information answering unasked questions that are too heavy for him to carry.

I suspected that since my father was in such complete denial I would probably be the logical person to answer my sister's painful question about death, but I remember standing there, emotionally and physically exhausted, wondering where I'd find the strength to handle this confrontation.

I took a deep breath, asked God to give me wisdom, and quietly began with, "Well, Marilyn, honey, if Mother had been in a car accident with both legs broken, ribs cracked, and stitches taken on the cuts, and you asked if she'd get better—I'd say, 'Yes, in time. In fact, by all we know of her injuries it shouldn't be too long.' But when I looked at all the signposts and symptoms on Mother today with breast cancer I have to say—no, honey, she is going to die."

Her eyes were just blazing with anger and she said, "She's not going to die. She's going to get well. God promised me Mother would be well." I felt I'd utterly failed with her. I was tired, mad at my father's refusal to see what was happening, and now to face the same denial from my sister snapped all the pins loose on my emotions. I just screamed at her—*"Mother is dying."*

"No, she's not," Marilyn sobbed. "Besides, how can you be so sure?"

"I just told you—by the signs," I yelled back.

"But God promised me He'd make her well. He promised—He promised," she countered back at me.

I went out in the hall, determined to leave her alone with her denial—but I couldn't go through with that so I asked God to somehow give me the right words for this delicate moment. I knew I had to bring this painful issue to a truthful conclusion. I whispered, "Lord, help!" and went back into the bedroom.

"Marilyn, do you remember when David was born?"

She turned her face to me. "Yes," she said.

"Well, I want to tell you something I've never told anyone else. When I saw David, I took one look at that beautiful baby and I said, 'Oh, Lord—make him well.' Marilyn, honey, God answered my prayer in *exactly* the way I hoped He would, but I never dreamed what He really meant. I only knew He promised me David would be well. I didn't know He meant *in heaven*—and not here on earth!

"Marilyn, it is possible that when God promised you Mother would be well—He meant heaven and not Reseda, California."

I'm sure she was fiercely angry with me, but she was tired and hurt by all the conflicts so I left her lying on the bed, covered with the blankets of her newly found grief.

I left her alone so she could begin to face the unalterable fact that Mother was not "holding her own and resting," but was, in all probability, dying.

My time with Marilyn that day was used of God, but my repeated tries with my father's denial gained no such success!

My anger toward Dad's denial was really catching hold of me because not only was I unable to understand it, but I was (by this time) terribly sick of dying. I was angry, too, at God for letting time drag my mother in and out of one pain-filled day after another.

Out of the blue, one day at the hospital, I got to wondering, "Where in the world are all the wonderful people from my father's church?" None of them had visited Mother and hardly any had sent flowers or other messages. It wasn't like them to be aloof—they were warm, loving people.

One morning I left the hospital to come home for a few hours. About noon I thought I'd call Mother's room and just check things with a nurse—if one answered. The phone was answered instantly and a familiar voice, but not my mother's or a nurse's, answered.

"Dottie? Dottie, is that you? This is Joyce," I said. There was a long silence on the other end, but I knew it was Dottie, one of the women from Dad's church. Finally, she whispered into the phone, "Joyce, this is awful—your mother is dying."

"Yes—I know," I answered. Dottie then said, "Last night I was praying and having devotions and the Lord said, *Go see Marion.*" But she argued with the Lord that Pastor Miller (my dad) had told the congregation there was nothing seriously wrong. All Marion needed was rest, and he asked them not to visit her as they might tire her. She'd called my sister and had been told, "Mother's holding her own."

"But," Dottie continued, "this morning the Lord told me again to see Marion, so I came. I'm sorry if I wasn't supposed to, but Joyce—she *is* dying."

I told her Dad was unable to face the fact of Mother's dying and that I was relieved that she knew. I asked her to go back to the church and tell the people the truth. I also requested that they pray her death would be soon because she was in tremendous pain.

I didn't go back to the hospital all that day. I was very depressed about Dad not admitting to himself, or anyone, the reality of Mother's condition. Late that night, when I was at my lowest point, the phone rang and it was Dad calling from the hospital. His message was just one, unbelievable line: "Mother's sinking fast—come quickly."

Leaving my husband with our children, I drove at neck-breaking speeds toward the hospital. I thought, "We've come from 'All she needs is soup and vitamins' to 'She's sinking fast.'" I was relieved. I thought, "Finally, Dad's facing the situation as it really is."

Mother had suffered a slight heart attack. Her heart was still fibrillating quite a bit even by the time I got there. My father was a picture of peace, but for once he did not tell me, "She's just fine." He told me how he had just sung to her. (She must have loved that —my dad has a beautiful voice, and over thirty-five years before, his voice and his violin playing were the first things that had made Mother fall in love with him.) He sang, "Good-bye, Our God Is Watching O'er You."

All through the night we sat with her and then my dad, no longer in denial, prayed a beautiful prayer. My notes only tell the last lines. He ended his prayer with an attempt to bargain. He said, "Let her see the morning light—if it be Thy will. And we shall praise Thee forever—amen."

By dawn her heartbeat was fairly normal, her color not too gray, and the crisis had passed. However, with the passing of the crisis so passed out the window my dad's acceptance and he went right back into his whistling, key-jangling denial.

Late that afternoon he was telling my sister that Mother had passed the crisis and now she'd be well. I don't remember what I said—and for sure I didn't take notes—but I do remember standing in the hall and telling him in a hundred different ways that what he'd just told Marilyn was *not true.*

I know I begged him to snap out of his irrational behavior. I treated him like he was a spoiled child stamping his foot for candy. I put him down very hard that day with verbal slaps.

After I had spent all my anger on him, he very quietly walked over to where Marilyn was standing. He put one arm around her shoulders and, facing me, said very directly, "I only have *one* daughter."

I deserved the remark. I wish I'd stood aside and let Dad's denial run its course. I just couldn't get it through my head that it was something he couldn't help.

I wish, too, I had had some magic way—some type of TV future replay—that would have made it possible to view him two weeks after my mother's death. I would have known the exact moment denial was dropped.

Dad went up north after Mother's funeral to spend a few days with old friends. One night he couldn't sleep so he dressed and went walking out in walnut groves. He was walking down a moonlit lane between the trees when suddenly he remembered something interesting that had happened that day. He just stopped and said out loud, "Oh, I must remember to tell Marion about that when I get home." And then for the first real, heart-piercing time, he realized she was not at home—she would never be at home—she was gone. He crumpled down beside one of those old walnut trees, stayed there, and cried until dawn.

Had I been able to have foreseen that time for him, I could have given him so much more patient love. I'm still sad over my ignorance that caused so much unnecessary friction between us.

My notebook reads, a few days later:

Doctor C. said, "Medically speaking, your mother should have died during that last crisis."

Doctor F. told Cliff, "She doesn't have months—maybe weeks, but, personally, I think only days."

The Red Cross extended Cliff's leave.

Last night both Cliff and I were there. Mother's fluid must have been building rapidly because she started to become irrational. To calm her I asked her if I could read to her. She insisted we both go. Her breathing was very difficult. Before we left she must have been in great pain (or perhaps she's tired of waiting, too) because she pulled me down close to her mouth and said, "Joyce, pray—pray."

On the elevator I said to Cliff, "How much longer can this continue?" He just shrugged his shoulders.

We are all so tired.

The next day I met the hospital's chaplain. I'd missed him on his other visits to Mother, but his face lit up when I introduced myself.

"So you're Marion Miller's *Joyce!* Oh, she's talked of you and your work—your singing and your radio program—I feel like I know you!"

Immediately after we talked, I picked up my pad so I'd remember what he said—exactly. My notes read:

Chaplain H.—"I go to see your mother quite often to give her a little lift, but each time I come away with the biggest lift for myself. You know, Joyce, your mother is not afraid to die. The death of a Christian like your mother is so beautiful. Just think—try to picture—your mother and her joy on entering heaven. Think, too, on all the joy *they* will have in welcoming her. I imagine she won't be there very long before someone says, 'Marion—I'm here because of you!' "

My dear chaplain, you were a beautiful ray of hope and returned momentarily my sanity to me after all those weeks. I don't know where you are right now, but, knowing God *does*, I've asked Him to bless your life in a special way right this minute.

My friend, Ruth Calkin, lost both her father and mother within a few short months of each other and penned:

Lord,
If like a fragile flower
Torn petal by petal
My heart must continue to tear,
Let there be fragrance.

In those painful weeks of waiting, I felt sure there would be no fragrance, and no worthwhile aroma out of all of it. I was wrong.

I did not know it then, but we had one more week to go. One more week of waiting, watching, and learning for us, and seven more days—168 hours—of excruciating pain for her. It was as an old TV show was entitled, "The Week That Was!"

However, the fragrance that was crushed out of that wild, marvelous week still swirls around me, filling my lungs with its pungent and savory memories.

It is enough to last—*regardless and always!*

7

Death and the Sound of Music

The wicked is overthrown by this
mischief-making, but the righteous,
while dying, has confidence.

PROVERBS 14:32 MLB

Andraé Crouch's contagious song "I Got Confidence" was probably
not written to sing around the beds of the dying, but for the dying
Christian I can hardly think of a better one to sing!

During the last week of my mother's life, we could distinctly feel
her God-given confidence in dying. Even though she did not always
understand the ways and workings of God, she spent that last week
alive and in great beauty. The dignity of her inner confidence was
apparent to all who saw her.

The week was filled with lessons Mother wanted desperately to
teach. She did not know the exact time of death, but she could hear
the rustle of the death angel's wings and knew it would be soon.

She dozed and slept like the dying usually do and then suddenly, remembering the urgency of the moment, she'd say something important and then instantly return to her sleep.

The dying are like babies who need large amounts of sleep. I liked watching the peaceful sleep which eased her, for a few moments now and then, out of her pain.

My grandmother and aunt had been vacationing in the East, but as soon as they reached home they hurried over to the hospital. They had left my mother in fairly good health, but now they saw her—weak, weighing about eighty pounds, and dying.

Just as they were visiting her, my mother had a slight heart attack. The doctors, nurses, and staff flew into the room and hurriedly ushered out the relatives—but not before my grandmother had her say.

She had taken a good look at all the equipment, IV bottles, and activity surrounding my mother, and angrily she startled the nearest doctor with, "Vy you do this? You stop. You let her go. You no keep her here. She ready to see God." My aunt hustled her out the door before Grandma could throttle the young doctor.

My grandmother's confidence was strong and steady. She thought it was terrible to prolong life, to keep Marion here and hold her back from heaven.

A little later one of the hospital attendants took my aunt aside and asked her who the older lady was. My aunt explained it was Marion's mother.

"Oh, dear!" The attendant seemed shocked. "It's a mistake to have such an elderly lady here. Does she know of her daughter's condition? Does she know she's terminal?" she asked.

"Yes," my aunt assured her.

"Then you should take her home. It's too hard on the aged to see their children die. Take her home."

My aunt wisely answered, "No—I'm not taking her home just yet. It's not wrong that she's here. You see, you don't know her, but I can tell you one thing—she's a praying mother. If my sister died and I hadn't let Mother see her, she would have spent the rest of her life saying to me, 'You didn't tell me about Marion—so I didn't pray —maybe God would have spared her life.' This way," my aunt continued, "our mother has been told, she has seen Marion, has prayed, and now she's left it up to God."

"I see," murmured the attendant. But I wonder if she really did.

My grandmother had taken stock of the whole hospital scene, and *knowing* God was about to take her daughter, accepted it without reservations. She had prayed and now it was up to God.

Not only the righteous, while dying, have confidence—but the people who stand by have a goodly share of it too!

My mother survived the crisis of that day and by the next morning was back to dozing, sleeping, and occasionally talking.

The next morning the lady bringing in the breakfast tray broke into a wide grin when she saw Mother.

"Hello, Mrs. Miller—how are you today?" Without waiting for a reply she continued, "Are you going to be a good girl and eat your breakfast?"

Mother smiled and said, "I'm really not hungry, but for you—I'll try."

The attendant stopped her well-developed chatter for sick patients and gently touched Mother's face.

I loved watching the scene because her touch shared the unspoken feeling of caring and my mother responded with, "Thank you—I hope you have a wonderful day today."

The woman glanced up at me and I could see she was deeply touched by a dying patient advising *her* to have a good day. She left with tears brimming in her eyes.

I put the spoon to Mother's mouth, but after one small bite she said, "Please, no more. It sticks right here in my throat and it won't go down."

I quit the feeding routine and asked her if I could read to her. She smiled and looked toward her nightstand where a new translation of the New Testament was lying.

She didn't have any preference so I just flipped the Bible open and began reading Colossians 2:1.

Somewhere about the seventh verse, I realized I was not reading alone.

"Mother, have you memorized this entire chapter?" (She'd not missed a word.)

"Oh, yes—" she said. "This is an exciting chapter!"

"But it's a brand new translation—it's hardly been published but a few months—and you already know it?" I was stunned.

We finished the chapter together with my reading and her reciting. Her sense of wonder at the promises of God was just as great as her sensitivity to the hospital attendant.

If the dying do not have the sense of wonder, then death becomes something horrible. For without God's positive reinforcement of love, death becomes a long tunnel that ends with a brick wall instead of an opening.

Later that day, she opened her eyes, looked at me, and said, "You know, honey, there are worse things to die of than this [she patted her chest]—" From all the suffering I'd seen related to breast cancer, I wasn't too sure I agreed with her. But I asked, "Like what?"

"Well," she answered, "you know—you could die of loneliness, like the kind the newly divorced suffer from or—" she paused— "worse yet, you could die alone—without God." She settled down deeply into her pillow. "Yes," she sighed, "that would be the *worst* death possible."

Our conversation was interrupted by a short visit from a friend. As Mother talked I was going to rub her with some lotion, but the friend took the bottle from me and gently massaged the lotion into my mother's cracked and drying hands.

Later, but not many minutes after the woman had gone, I had this conversation with my mother:

"Joyce!"

"Yes, Mother—"

"Why was she so tender to me?"

"She knows you don't have long, Mother." There was a pause. "Joyce?"

"Yes—"

"Promise me something?"

"I promise. What do you want?"

"I want you to promise me you will never stop praying for her. You know she needs the Lord."

"Yes, I know—I promise, Mother."

"Remember now, no matter how hopeless you feel she is—don't give up. She must not die—alone—without God—without Him. Promise?"

"I promise, Mother."

It was an interesting lesson. There she lay dying a very painful death of breast cancer, but wanting me to know that dying without God was infinitely *worse*. By asking me to pray for the woman, she gave me another project to take myself out of grief's self-centeredness and into positive actions relating to others. (Smart lady, my mother.)

On the second day of that last week I caught on to another lesson. While she was no construction engineer, she gave me some unique bridge-building instructions. Carefully she began gathering materials, for she wanted to leave me with a well-built bridge. The bridge was to be made of one important message and she wanted it to span the time between when she died and when we'd all meet again in heaven. She constructed her bridge by using three words over and over again. Building went on at all hours of the day and night.

"Joyce?"

"Yes, Mother."

"Are you still here?"

"Mmmm."

"What are you doing over there?"

"Nothing—I'm just being."

"Is it night or morning?"

"It's 2:30 in the morning, Mother."

"Joyce?"

"Yes."

"I love you."

"I love you too—Mother."

Another time, just as I was leaving her room, she called out and built another section to her bridge with, "Honey?"

"Yes, Mother."

"Are you leaving or going away?"

"Well, not really—I'm just going to get a cup of coffee downstairs."

"Oh—go ahead."

I had just stepped into the hall when I heard her add, "Joyce—you are loved." She was doing a beautiful yet strange thing. As nearly as I could tell she was building a bridge with the words "I love you" toward us, yet, at the very same time, she was slowly detaching herself from us. She was loving us while she was cutting the ties. Generally the verbal words "I love you" were followed by the silent, unspoken word *Good-bye*. Each of us was to hear her words of love and her farewells.

Many other people have shared with me their conversations with the dying. They tell me the words "I love you" are said and emphatically repeated over and over again.

I find it very moving that after all is said, experienced, and done, the words "I love you" end up being the most important words left to say.

When Marilu's young son was injured in a bicycle accident, he underwent two brain surgeries to relieve hemorrhaging. In the hours that followed he was only conscious for a few seconds, but before he died he gave his most important message when he called, "Mama . . . Mama?" Marilu touched his arm and said, "I'm right here, honey." He responded with, "Oh, Mama, I love you." The dying *know* and they want "I love you" to be remembered.

On the third day of the last week my mother taught me about a Christian's sense of humor.

I had left her room while she was dozing. The cafeteria was almost empty. I was too late for breakfast and too early for lunch so I had two cups of coffee and their last rather stale doughnut.

When I came back to Mother's room it didn't register that the door might be closed for a reason—I just pushed on through and there I froze in my tracks from what I saw.

My mother was turned on her side, her back toward me, and two nurses were on the other side of the bed facing her and holding her hands. Two doctors at Mother's back were intently inserting ugly-looking drainage tubes. Large bottles on the floor were hooked up with the tubes and the doctors had just begun the procedure. (It's called a thoracentesis—or pumping treatment to drain the fluid out of the chest cavity.) While she had received this treatment other times during the past year, I'd certainly never seen it and I'd never been allowed into the room while it was being done. I said, "Whoops—I'm sorry—" and started to back out the door.

"Don't go—I want you to sit right there and watch this." The senior doctor so ordered and I sat.

"Is he kidding?" I thought. "Why does he want me to see this?" My mother's hands were being held by the two nurses and she was gripping them hard because of the pain and her knuckles showed white through the taut skin.

After the doctor had adjusted the tubes once more, he straightened up and announced sternly and abruptly, "Joyce—I never want to see you in this place as a patient with advanced breast cancer." He put his hand gently on my mother's back— "She knew she had lumps and she waited too long. This—" he waved his hands over the bottles, tubes, and paraphernalia of the dying—"this is needless! We could have saved her, but she waited too long." He was very emotional—I loved him deeply in those moments because he dropped the cold, professional mask and spoke to me as a human being concerned, in great loving care, about another human being. He was in his middle thirties, around six feet, three inches tall, and the most handsome black doctor I'd ever seen. He was completely enchanted by my fifty-seven-year-old mother. (The morning my mother died he said, "I've only known her for the past few months —I wish to God I'd known her my whole lifetime like you have.")

He called her, "Mrs. Miller-honey" and while he was asking me if I had regular checkups Mother said, "Doctor, tell her again—I waited too long."

"I am, Mrs. Miller-honey, I am," he answered. (This year thirty-two thousand women will die of breast cancer and many of their deaths could have been prevented by early detection.)

I sat there for another fifteen minutes and then the doctor asked me to take the nurses' place and hold Mother's hands. I came around the bed and was met by the plainly visible force of her agony. There well may be a treatment procedure which is more painful, but I sincerely doubt it. She managed a very wan smile and asked, "Is it almost over? Are they almost through?" I looked across her at the doctors—together they shook their heads, indicating negative. "It will be just a little bit more," I lied.

Pretty soon her face lit up and I knew she'd had some kind of an inspiration. She said, "Joyce, honey, sing for me!"

Without looking up I could see the doctors behind her—just staring at me. "What did you say, Mother?" I asked.

"Sing for me right now. It will help the time to go faster."

I was still a little surprised and was about to tell her I had practically no voice at all when her doctor said, "Oh, Mrs. Miller-

honey—Joyce has been here almost seven weeks around the clock—
she's so tired—she probably can't sing—don't ask her to."

My mother's old, vivacious personality and vibrant sense of
humor just snapped, crackled, and popped through her brown eyes.
She turned her head backward just enough to see them and said,
"Listen here—Doctor-honey—if you paid for as many voice lessons
as I have—when I say sing—*she sings!*" The room exploded with
laughter.

"Atta girl, Mrs. Miller-honey—atta girl!" they said in unison to her.
"*Sing!*" they said to me.

It was during her greatest moments of unbelievable pain that she
came through with her giant sense of humor.

Long before those moments at her bedside she had taught me
not to take myself too seriously. She did not want me to come unglued over the way life was shaping up for me. What was happening to me in my little world was important, she said, but not earth-
shaking.

Now she was dying and in prolonged pain, but she knew how it
would all end and she had God's confidence. She knew how it
would all work out and she didn't want anyone to take all of this
too seriously.

I can still hear, in my memory's ear, the doctors who all day said,
"Did you hear what Mrs. Miller-honey said today?"

I could hardly refuse her request so I said, "Okay, what do you
want me to sing?"

I was dead tired, with very little voice left, and I didn't want to
sing. I felt like the captured people of Israel David wrote about in
one of his psalms.

Weeping, we sat beside the rivers of Babylon thinking of Jerusalem.
We have put away our lyres, hanging them upon the branches of the
willow trees, for how can we sing?

Psalms 137:1–3

"Good question," I thought. "How can I sing?" But as I stood
there looking at Mother's face and seeing her bravery and courageous stamina I thought, "I'd better *find* the voice to sing because
if she can endure these tubes suctioning out the fluid in her chest

with such good humor and love, the least I can do is sing my heart out for her! Besides, there *was* the matter of all those voice lessons!"

Before she told me what she wanted me to sing, I would have guaranteed anyone that she would ask for either the song, "His Eye Is on the Sparrow" or, "My Heavenly Father Watches Over Me."

She looked up, however, and said, "Oh, honey, sing *The Sound of Music.*"

"The song or the whole thing?" I asked. She answered, "The *whole* thing!"

I certainly hadn't expected that.

But there in that hospital room—with doctors, nurses, tubes, equipment, and even cleaning women—I sang the whole musical while she held tightly to my hands.

The windows had been opened and a slight ocean breeze was drifting across the room. When I got to the last song, she lifted her head, ever so slightly, toward the windows and the cool air seemed to gently fan her with fresh life. She bravely and majestically sang the last four lines with me:

> I go to the hills when my heart is lonely,
> I know I will hear what I've heard before,
> My heart will be blessed with the sound of music
> And I'll sing once more.

As we sang, the realization swept over my soul that she didn't *need* the assurance or the comfort of such beautiful gospel songs as "His Eye Is on the Sparrow" because she was already assured and comforted by God's love.

No wonder she asked for *The Sound of Music*—she wanted to hear songs that would be a prologue to her homegoing. She knew she was soon to hear all the magnificent voices, choirs, and instruments of heaven. She wanted me to sing the opening preludes and to start the earthly overture for the great heavenly concert that was about to begin for her.

Much later that day, when the doctors had removed the tubes and taken away the bottles filled with fluid, Mother was not better as everyone had hoped. In fact, she had lost much strength.

Patiently she adjusted to her new weakness and at one point her adjustment was remarkable. She said, "Joyce—push here—push here." I couldn't figure out what she meant by "push" and she was so weak she could barely communicate. With great effort she said, "Push your head down here—we'll wait together." She had tried to say "put"—but it came out "push." Finally I understood and I put my head next to hers and we waited together.

I didn't sleep too well because she was breathing in the extraordinary way the dying do with long, scary pauses between breaths.

It was most frightening to be listening to her steady, normal breathing and then to hear nothing but silence. The seconds would fly away and mount up in what felt like years and then—she'd simply resume breathing. Once I really panicked and ran to find the nearest doctor. When I asked him what was happening to Mother, he muttered something about it not being too unusual and left me standing in the hall, knee-deep in unanswered, fearful questions.

Later on that morning I saw a dear friend of mine and I was telling her how scary it was to listen to Mother breathing because I was never sure if it was her last breath.

Bettye will never know the exact measure of my relief when I heard her say, "Oh, yes, I know about that breathing process. She must be breathing the Cheyenne-Stokes way. My father did that too."

"What's *Cheyenne-Stokes?*" I asked.

She spent the next few minutes telling about the two doctors (Cheyenne and Stokes) who had discovered this kind of breathing problem in the dying and had done research on it.

I wondered why the doctor, when I asked him about Mother's unusual breathing, had brushed the questions off as unimportant. Why didn't he tell me that, for her, it *was* normal? It wouldn't have been nearly so frightening to me if he had even briefly explained about her respiratory centers being so badly affected by the disease that they were not responding normally, so her breathing *would* be highly irregular. I suppose, though, it's hard for doctors and nurses —working day after day in medicine—to understand that lay people are simply nowhere near as knowledgeable as they. Or that what may be a common occurrence to a doctor who has seen the problem —if not in patients, at least in textbooks—may be a terribly foreign and frightening experience for people trying to cope with death and dying.

I will always be grateful to Pinkey, a friend and a nurse, who patiently answered my frantic phone calls when Mother's condition would change. If I didn't understand what was happening, I'd call Pinkey and she'd give me the answers I needed. It was always easier to cope when I knew *what* it was I was trying to cope with. It was the same way with my friend Bettye's explanation of the breathing. It helped remove the paralyzing effects of fear in my own heart as I waited with my mother. Once I understood the Cheyenne-Stokes breathing, it was relatively easy to accept the phenomenon later when it occurred over and over again. I did not panic.

The fourth day came and went uneventfully, but on the fifth day of that week Mother quietly but determinedly announced, "I want to go home." She made her request to everyone and by the time she asked her favorite "Doctor-honey," to my surprise, "Doctor-honey" said, "Your mother wants to go home. I'll release her to go home for twenty-four to forty-eight hours, depending on how long she wants to stay, and then you'll have to bring her back."

We all scurried around, readied up the house, rented an oxygen tank, breathing apparatus called "The Bird," and other equipment and, finally, borrowed a friend's new station wagon. We gently placed her on foam-rubber pads and took her home that afternoon.

My brother and Dad brought her into the house amid much laughing and fun scolding. It was a welcome release of tensions to laugh and she helped us all by winking at me and saying, "I know they're gonna drop me!" They managed to not fulfill the prediction, but placed her on an outdoor chaise lounge which had wheels on it.

I think it was exactly at that moment we realized why it was so important to her to come home. She wanted to say a meaningful, proper good-bye to all of us.

Almost seven weeks before she had left her home, left us, left her furniture and things, even left her favorite little dog, Buttons, fully expecting to be home in a few days. Now she knew she'd be leaving forever and she wanted to say her loving farewells to all of us, surrounded by the familiarity of her earthly home.

"Mother," I said, "you want to go into all the rooms, don't you?"

"Oh, yes—take me," she responded.

So we pushed her down the hall past bedrooms and bathroom

long enough for her to glimpse inside each room and whisper her faint good-byes. Then we turned her around, pushed her back down the hall, let her stay in the center of her kitchen for a few minutes, and then rolled her narrow bed into the dining room.

For a moment she looked at her dish cabinet and then, longingly, she looked outside through the sliding glass doors toward the swimming pool we had all had so much fun in and around.

"You want to go out there, too?" I asked. She quickly nodded yes.

The September sun was broiling the backyard plants to dry crispiness, but she lay out there for a few minutes letting its penetrating heat warm up her death-chilled bones. When she was ready we took her back inside, through the dining room to the living room, and as we got to the piano she said, "Stop." Then looking at my sister she said, "Marilyn, honey, I want you to play one more song for me."

The circle of farewells was now completed. She had said her good-byes to all of us, to the rooms, and even to the swimming pool of the house, and now even the last of the songs had been sung. With the exception of my brother (who is not too terribly musical) all of us had sung for her. My singing of *The Sound of Music,* my father's songs to her weeks before, and now my sister's note-perfect classical piano playing had completed the sounds of earth and she asked to be taken to the den so she could rest.

Darkness came to the San Fernando Valley that night and we fixed up some blankets on the floor beside Mother's bed. My brother and I worked out a schedule where one of us would be awake with her the whole night. We alternated every two hours. Around five or six in the morning I sent my brother off to bed and took my third or fourth shift. We didn't turn on any lights, we just came and went all during the night.

My mother seemed to be sleeping quietly so I lay back on my blankets waiting for daybreak and wondering what new sadness the day would bring.

Suddenly her hand came tapping down my arm, back up again toward my neck and face, and I heard her say, "Who's down there? Who do I have *now?*"

"It's me—Joyce," I answered, and her humor flickered for a

moment because she chuckled a bit and said, "I wasn't sure—you know—there's been a lot of coming and going around here lately!"

We both lay there in the faint light of the new dawn breaking onto the world that day and then from the stillness her voice said, calmly and with no apparent breathing difficulties, "Joyce, I'm going home. Soon."

"Yes, Mother—just think—you'll see Jesus."

"Not soon enough. I want to go *now*, honey."

"I know, Mother—I know."

She drifted off to sleep. Later, when the room was lighter, I saw her hand as it came down off the bed and groped for my shoulder. She tapped me and said, "If that's still you, Joyce—*pray!*"

Not only did the sun dawn on us that morning, the sixth day of her last week—but dawning on me came the horrible realization I had a speaking engagement that noon. I had not cancelled it because it was so far into September I was sure by then I'd be back on schedule again. However, I'd completely forgotten it. I don't know why I remembered it, other than the Lord had wanted me to go. I sat up, touched her face, and told Mother that I was supposed to speak for her local Christian Businesswoman's Club luncheon. I asked her if she minded if I left her and went. She urged me to go and her mind was clear enough to tell me to say hello to Frances Eliers, who would be there. Reluctantly I got up and left her to get dressed. When I was all ready to leave I went in to see if she was all right. She said she needed a bedpan so I took care of her needs and was leaving the room, all dressed up for a luncheon and carrying out her used bedpan, when she looked up, smiled, and said, "Ah, yes, you should write a book called *From Bedpan to Banquet* by Joyce Landorf." The humor of it helped me go. I do not remember what I spoke on or even if I sang (I doubt it), but since the luncheon was a local chapter and my mother attended regularly I remember many of her personal friends coming to the head table to tell me of their love and prayers. So many did not preach or fumble for words; they simply said, "I love her, too." Their words gave the most marvelous uplift to my dragging spirits.

I drove back to my parents' house after the luncheon and my aunt and grandmother were there. It was a scene I'll never forget.

My grandmother was sitting on the edge of the bed holding my mother's hand and my aunt was just standing there when this conversation took place. It was in Hungarian, but what I didn't understand my aunt filled in for me.

My grandmother said, "Mutishka (Marion) my daughter, are you dying?"

Mother nodded her head yes.

"Mutishka, are you afraid of death?"

Mother gave a slight smile and said, "No, Mama."

Grandma stood up and said, "Good. I give her to God. I go now." Then she picked up her little black hat, jammed it down on the top of her head, pinned it with a hatpin like all little old ladies do, and said to my aunt, "Come—we go now. We wait at home." Looking at me she said, "You call me when she go."

Ah, that confidence again! Long after she left that day my mother's mouth showed the traces of a smile because of that dear conversation.

My sister, Marilyn, and my daughter, Laurie, were at the house and I asked them to try not to cry when they were with Mother. I was fiercely protective of Mother and I knew it would be terribly upsetting to her if both girls really gave way to their tears. However, my lecture didn't work too well because when Laurie (then eleven) took one look at her very beloved grandmother, her whole face gave her way—she fled into the other room to sob her heart out.

Mother said, "What in the world is the matter with Laurie—I couldn't get a word out of her." I explained that Laurie's love for her was very deep and that in seeing her she had realized her grandmother was going to heaven soon—and it was too much for her. Mother just smiled a knowing smile. Then my sister came in. Mother took the matter of her death into her own hands and she said, "Marilyn, honey, this disease will not heal. I'm not going to get well." My sister, unable to hold the flow of tears back—in spite of my instructions—put her head down on Mother's stomach and just sobbed out the burning question, "Mother, Mother, why is God doing this?" My mother very firmly, but quietly, answered, "I don't know, honey, I don't know." The two stayed there without moving or talking and the stillness of that hour was broken only by my sister's muffled sobbing.

We may all find ourselves in the place of not knowing or understanding the whys of death, but it is important to realize that when Mother said, "I don't know," she said it without fear, without bitterness, and without frustration. Her words, spoken so long ago, have tenderly touched my heart to this day. There is so much in this world we don't know or understand so it is not a question of having *all* the answers at our fingertips, but rather entrusting to God our painful whys and then watching His quiet peace erase the fear, bitterness, and frustrations from the blackboards of our minds.

When my mother gave God her whys He had not answered them, but had given, instead, a genuine measure of peaceful confidence to tide her over. It was enough for her then and it remains enough for my sister and for all of us now.

That day she not only showed us that a Christian dies in quiet confidence, but that a Christian dies with forgiveness up to date. She had been dozing later that afternoon when she suddenly woke up and startled me with, "Joyce, have I been a good mother to you?" The question was such an easy one to answer that I laughed out loud at the turn the conversation had taken. "Oh, Mother," I said rather joyfully, "you have been the kind of mother whose children rise up and call her *blessed!* All of us—Cliff, Marilyn, Dick—wo all call you blessed and for the rest of our lives we will always remember just how wonderful you were as a mother."

But she was not smiling—in fact, she was shaking her head slowly and forming the words, "No—that's not true.

"Joyce," she said, "I've failed you and Dick."

"No—no," I protested. "If you have, I can't remember it and if you did fail, it doesn't matter now!" I thought I was shushing her up, but she would not be shushed.

"I failed you at least once, I remember," she said. "I failed you when David died—I didn't come to the funeral. Remember?" Without letting me say anything, she plunged right on: "I made a terrible mistake then, Joyce, I should have been there. Honey, will you forgive me for not going to little David's funeral?"

"Oh, Mother," I was crying, "I already have forgiven you—so long ago—I was hurt by Daddy and you not coming, but finally I was able to stop trying to forgive and I let God work forgiving through me. It's all been done and it's all right." The beauty of the

moment was incredible. It takes *very large* parents to admit to their
child that *they* were wrong, or to accept the blame, but it takes a
supergiant parent to follow these admissions with the words, "Will
you forgive me?" But she wanted to die with old hurts healed and
her own forgiveness brought up to date—as she felt was fitting for
a Christian.

It was near evening when her breathing, even with the help of
the machines, was going badly. She was obviously distressed and
unable to get sufficient air into her lungs.

Her words rasped out to me: "Joyce, how are you praying for
me?"

There was no way I was about to tell her *exactly* how I was
praying. It would have sounded too cold and too unloving. Not
only was I praying a certain way, but many people at that time
were. Her physical agony and pain were lasting beyond anyone's
concept of endurance, so we were all praying that God would
take her home. "Pray that it will be today," we agreed. On the surface that kind of praying seems and sounds rather insensitive. However, it's not—in view of all the symptoms of dying—it's really the
only prayer to pray. But I found I was unable to tell her the truth
and by then I had hesitated so long she asked again, "Tell me, how
are you praying?"

Deliberately lying, I said, "Well, I'm praying that the Lord's
will be done."

A look of complete disgust passed across her face and with a
great deal of scorn in her voice she rebuked me with, "Well, you
stop that prayer this instant! That's the wrong way to pray!"

"It is?" I meekly replied.

"It certainly is. You ask the Lord to take me home. This—" she
began coughing—"this has gone on too long." She took several deep
breaths from the oxygen mask and then finished with, "Tell Him to
hurry up—I'm past due!"

I don't know if she sensed I'd lied about the content of my
prayers, but it was for sure she wanted me to know she was dying
in truth—not wrapped up and protected by sincere, well-meaning
lies—but dying in unhypocritical honesty. She also knew it was
time to leave and she wanted me to stop hindering her homegoing.

After she had taught me her lesson on how to pray for the dying, she dismissed me by falling asleep.

Later when she awoke I asked her if she wanted me to read to her. She said, "Yes, something from Philippians."

I opened to Philippians and asked, "Any particular place, Mother?" She lifted her hand in a gesture that said it didn't matter —so I looked down and read the first line I saw:

But whatever happens to me, remember always to live as Christians should, so that, whether I ever see you again or not, I will keep on hearing good reports that you are standing side by side with one strong purpose—to tell the Good News fearlessly, no matter what your enemies may do.

Philippians 1:27

She put her hand over the page so I looked at her. She was smiling—she said, "I'll be listening for all those good reports!" Then she motioned for me to begin reading again.

After I'd read verse thirty of the same chapter, she said, "No more."

I'd read, "We are in this fight together. You have seen me suffer for him in the past; and I am still in the midst of a great and terrible struggle now, as you know so well" (Philippians 1:30).

I took notes that afternoon and the last line on my scribbled page was written after I'd read Philippians. I wrote:

Oh, yes, dear Mother, I've seen you suffering, but always you have been utterly fearless! Thank God for His confidence.

Late that afternoon I met with my brother in the long hall outside her door. We discussed her breathing, which was much worse, and decided it was time for her to go back to the hospital. I went into her room and asked her if she wanted to go back to the hospital and immediately she answered, "Yes—*now*."

My dad, brother, sister, and I were just getting her settled on the pads in the back of the station wagon when my father's sister and most of his family from Michigan pulled in the driveway. It was mass confusion because none of us had seen each other for years and Dad's letters had never told them the seriousness of Mother's illness, so they didn't know she was sick, much less dying.

In all the noisy confusion with aunts, uncles, and cousins, I bent over Mother and told her I would stay at home with the relatives and that I'd see her in the morning. As her mind registered what I was saying she angrily shook her head no. It was a positive, stubborn, authority-filled *no* and I couldn't understand why she said it with such angry vehemence.

I bent over and kissed her quickly and said, "Mother, it's all right. I'll see you in the morning. Aunt Ellen and Uncle Greg have come all this way and someone better stay with them. Okay?" She closed her eyes and didn't answer me. I wish I'd known what she knew at that moment—that sometimes the dying have no more I'll-see-you-in-the-mornings left.

They drove out of the driveway and I went in to explain to my shocked and saddened relatives that Mother had precious little time left.

I was still talking in the living room when they returned from the hospital. Dad reported Mother was settled and had bid them all good night and had even sent them on their way. I was just asking about her trip back to the hospital when the phone rang. It was for me—my husband, Dick, was calling to tell me that he did not want me to stay there or at the hospital that night and would I please come home. Our children needed me, he needed me, and he felt I needed to get some rest. We had a gentle argument, but in the end I knew he was probably right so I said I'd come home.

On the freeway the Santa Monica turnoff toward UCLA Medical Center loomed up in front of me—it was near midnight and there was no traffic. I almost turned off, but at the last second continued straight and drove home. It was good to see my home and husband again and to be in my own bed felt marvelous.

The first ring of the phone next to our bed brought us both up with a quick jerk. It was light in our room and not quite 7:00 A.M. Dick answered by the second ring. Without saying too much, he listened and then replaced the phone on its stand.

"That was Dad. The hospital said she died in her sleep this morning at 6:34."

"Thank God," breathed out of somewhere inside of me, but then as I was aware of the sunlight flooding our room, anguished thoughts screamed inside of me—"Oh, Mother—it's morning—and after all that waiting and watching—I didn't get to see you go! I wasn't there—and it's morning. You went without me—I wanted to be there—Oh, dear God, no! She knew she'd run out of mornings last night. She tried to tell me—but I didn't listen and I left her. I didn't see her go—I had *meant* to be there."

The knife of regret struck again and again and when there was nothing left to strike it stayed on stirring the slush of what was left of my heart.

Grandfather

He looked through me,
His eyes heavy with death.

He did not say, but wished to say:
    "Open the window."

So I opened the window
And turned to tell him
It was useless to try and drag himself
The impossible distance to where he might
Also look across the fields and fences
Toward the woods
Of his Sunday afternoon wanderings.

I turned to tell him
That birds were building new nests
Upon the sites of the old,
And that the little river had shifted again,
But Grandfather left me by the window
And went himself
To see about the things I meant to tell him.

ROBERT M. HOWELL

8

Majestic Mourning Song

Hush li'l' baby—don' you cry
You know your mama was born to die
All my trials Lord, soon be over.
All my trials Lord, soon be over.

Jordan river is chilly and cold,
Chills the body but not the soul,
All my trials Lord, soon be over.
All my trials Lord, soon be over.

TRADITIONAL SPIRITUAL

For those of us left behind to pick up the fragmented pieces of our broken lives—can there be any song to living? Will there ever be a time when our hearts do not feel the tearing and ripping apart that continues to splinter and smash them? Will we ever respond to others and to our daily routines in what we once knew as a normal way? Since the experience of losing to death is so devastating, the immediate answers to these questions seem to be no—unequivocally *no.*

Yet at the same instant we shout the answer, "No"—there is a spontaneous, almost involuntary motion of hope deep within us and somewhere we hear someone say, "Wait a minute, aren't you God's child? If you are, then hang on to this and grab hold of God's words.

He said, 'I'll not leave you comfortless.' Didn't He promise to help us walk this dark valley? Of course He did and now He has given His Word for our safe return to life and normalcy."

What God has promised, really, is to give us a song—even in the midst of death and sorrow. It will not be the frivolous, New Orleans jazz-band music that's played at funerals and wakes, but rather it will be a quiet song full of confidence. A song fitting enough for a bridal procession, exciting enough for a New Year's Day parade, and majestic enough for a king's coronation day! An orchestrated song for full symphony, and its incredible beauty will not disappear into the night, but will be heard forever.

We almost do not dare to listen. It sounds too good to be true and we think, "Music out of all of this?" We have lost and we have been sliced in half. We are alone and we feel abandoned. We cannot imagine being a whole person again. It is too much to believe in or hope for.

But God is not dead and when His children experience death and the sorrowing grief which follows, He begins His majestic mourning song. To hear it is to begin to breathe again. At first the song seems strange and remote, but it *is* there.

The morning my mother died I heard the song faintly, but it was drowned out by two pressing obligations:

1. A writing assignment: I was writing for the Biola College magazine and my column was past due. Other than I knew I should write about my mother's homegoing, I had no other creative words or ideas.

2. Funeral arrangements: Since my father was still in denial, he awaited me at his home. I was to come and make the necessary arrangements. I had little or no desire to do this and I was fatigued beyond belief.

Just as we were getting dressed and ready to go to Dad's house, I grabbed (almost absentmindedly) a piece of paper and a pen. Before I knew it these words appeared and flowed out on to the paper. To a background of grief's quiet music the column came and read like this:

Right now the angels of heaven are rushing through those golden corridors, shouting, "Marion is here, Marion is here!"

In my mind's eye I can see all of heaven assembling in the great hall. Angels, saints of the Old and New Testament, our Lord, and of course, the new one, Marion.

Marion, born in 1909 of such humble beginnings in a little village, east of Budapest, Hungary, brought to this country as a little girl, now stands in heaven!

I imagine she is impatient a little as she wants to join the choir. And join she will! It may take a few days for the director to figure it out, but soon he will complain to his superior music-master that, "Marion sings off key."

The complaint will reach the higher-ups and then the word will come back, "She must stay in the choir and yes, in the front row, even though she can't carry a tune."

"Why?" comes the gentle question of the director.

"Well, it seems for most of her 57 years on earth she has sung her praises to the Lord," is the reply.

She has introduced hundreds of children to the Master by her loving work in Sunday school, daily vacation Bible school, Child Evangelism classes and many summer weeks at "Good News" camps.

She has worked physically, mentally and spiritually side by side with her minister husband for almost 38 years, sharing all the joys and all the heartaches of the ministry.

She has been a mother whose three children "rise up and call her blessed."

By her exciting Bible classes and her chaplaincy in the Christian sorority, Lambda Theta Chi, she has helped countless women to trust in Christ. By her everyday living she has inspired even more men and women to give God only their very best.

Always she has sung her song of praise. (Yes, "off key." Sometimes she has changed keys nine times in one chorus of "In My Heart There Rings a Melody.") The Lord, however, says it is the sweetest sound He heard coming from earth so she is to continue her song in the choir as before. Heaven wouldn't be right without that sweet "off-key" voice.

The great hall is filled now, all of heaven has gathered, and the angels have finished their magnificent songs of praise and all are standing quietly, with folded wings, for they are listening to Marion.

What are the words to that beautiful song?

> Holy, Holy is what the angels sing,
> And I expect to help them make
> the courts of heaven ring.

> But when I tell redemption's story
> They will fold their wings.
> For angels never felt the joys
> That our salvation brings.

So with her gentle humor and her exciting way of talking she is telling them how she went from "sinner" to "saved" and all about the "joys of salvation brought."

Heaven glistens a little brighter today because Marion Miller, my mother, is there.

The Lord, in the moments it took to write those words, began His first move toward healing me. I started to hear His music. He helped me laugh as I reread the article, especially when He reminded me of my mother's inability to stay on tune. All the times I'd tried to imitate her, but couldn't, were flashed back through my mind and it was a warm, happy memory.

The warmth of the memory was short-lived because soon my husband and I left our home and made our way across Los Angeles to begin funeral arrangements.

My dad met us at his front door and then together we took our last journey to UCLA Medical Center. It was strange going there this time, and when I reached the third floor I automatically went straight into my mother's room. I was stunned and stopped short by the immaculate, sterile-looking room. The bed was newly made up and quite empty. The absence of not only a person, but all equipment, was mind boggling. The room was devoid of any human personality. It was just a very barren place, impersonal and cold. I must have experienced some of the same feelings the disciples of Jesus felt when they looked into the empty tomb. "He is not here, He is risen" (*see* Matthew 28:6 KJV), they were told. I know how blank their minds must have gone at that instant.

I leaned against the doorjamb and tried to figure it out. I finally thought, "She is not here—I wonder why I looked for her—she, too, is gone—she is with God."

I turned out of the doorway into the hall and bumped into Mother's favorite "Doctor-honey." All I could say was, "She's gone." My words were quiet with acceptance.

The doctor responded, "I didn't know—I wasn't in the ward this morning—I didn't know until now." He was crying as he talked. He apologized and said that tears were highly unprofessional, but he had loved Mrs. Miller-honey.

We stepped over to the desk and I filled in some things on several pieces of paper. We signed autopsy permission papers and because my mother spent her life giving to others, we signed papers giving her eyes to UCLA's famous eye bank. The last thing I wrote on one of those papers was her age. After the doctor looked at it he said, "Joyce, your mother was thirty-four?"

"Whoops—" I hastily corrected it to fifty-seven and said, "I don't know why I wrote down my own age instead of hers other than I always thought of us as being the same age." My mother had been a "becomer" as Keith Miller would have called her, had he known her. She was not an "arriver," or one who knew everything about anything with no more need to learn. She was young at heart and life was full of new adventures and new lessons to learn. Most often her conversation started out with, "Well, what new and wonderful thing has God done in your life today?" To think of her as not only fifty-seven years of age, but *gone* as well, was very difficult. Denial was easy.

Her body was somewhere in the hospital, but we did not see it that day.

I walked down the corridor listening to the sweet, sad symphony of my mourning song that was beginning to crescendo in my heart. There was no more reason to come to that place and, strange as it seems, I was bittersweet sad to leave it. The hospital had been my home for weeks. It had been kind to my mother—its staff had fallen in love with her. Even in dying she had reached out, in God's love, and transformed lives. She would not soon be forgotten—I was reluctant to leave when all was said and done.

After leaving the hospital, we went back to Dad's home to plan the funeral.

Much has been said about funerals in the past decade. The best that's been said about *Christians* and funerals, however, has been said by Joe Bayly in *The View From a Hearse* and by Gladys Hunt in her book *The Christian Way of Death*.

It is no wonder, though, that funeral arrangements are so baffling to most of us. We have just experienced the most frightening loss of our life and our minds are fragmented like so many pieces of shattered glass on a tile floor.

Suddenly we find, as much as we'd like to stay hidden within the confines of shock and denial, we must rouse ourselves and come forward. We must pick out a casket, get a dress or a suit over to the mortuary, and give out directions as to what type of service is best. However, these are just a few of the surface things that must be done. If the death is a sudden one, if there was no will, if all funds were in one name and not in a joint checking account, if all insurance papers were kept secret, you can see the horrendous amounts of red tape you'll have to work through, and all of this is on *top* of your grief.

When our son died I was still recovering in the hospital from the cesarean-section surgery so my husband had to make all of David's funeral arrangements.

Our local mortician was tremendously helpful. He knew of the huge medical expenses that were piling up so he made it easy for my husband by listing for him each price range (for casket, burial, etc.) and suggesting ways to cut funeral costs way down. We are still indebted to Todd's Mortuary for all the gentle kindnesses they extended to us.

Our experience a year later when my grandfather died, in another city, with a different mortuary, was exactly the opposite.

I accompanied my aunt to the mortuary to pick out a casket for Grandpa. The large, cold room (I don't know why it wasn't heated) filled with caskets was more frightening than a monster movie. Our nerves and emotions were ravaged as it was, but to stand amid twenty or thirty empty caskets was an experience not easily accepted. I could not take my eyes off a small blue-and-white baby's casket. It would have fit David so well. The pain of the moment penetrated my soul without mercy.

That pain was nothing, however, compared with the violent pain the mortician inflicted on our suffering souls. He was as jovial as a master of ceremonies for a festive banquet and twice as phony. In his pseudofriendly voice, he came up behind my aunt and said, "Well, now, how are we coming along?" Without waiting for a reply, he glanced at the casket my aunt was studying and said, "Oh, no, my dear, you don't want to put Papa in that *cheap* casket—put him in this one over here."

My first inner thought was that he had no right to call Grandpa "Papa"—it should be "Mr. Uzon" to him, but my second thought blurted out of me before I could stop it.

"How much *is* that 'cheap casket' we *don't* want for Papa?" He muttered something about it being nine hundred dollars and said again it wouldn't do for Papa.

I remember firmly taking my aunt's arm and (knowing Grandpa only had about one thousand dollars from insurance to bury himself) I told her, "I think that one will do very well for our beautiful Papa—because in the first place, he's not really *here*, but with the Lord; and, in the second place, he didn't have a ton of money."

My aunt was sick with grief and had no heart for discussing or haggling over prices and no one took more advantage of the situation than the mortician. I still experience feelings of anger when I remember how he made her feel obligated to buy the casket next higher in price.

Gladys Hunt summed up my feelings on funerals when she stated in *The Christian Way of Death:*

In the final analysis, a Christian funeral is not determined by cost or efficiency, but by the message it proclaims.

At the time of death there are so many factors that arise (and cost is certainly one of them), yet we must not lose sight of the message of life and hope we have as Christians. We must not fail to take into consideration the deceased's life, his attitudes and, yes, his economical position. A father's death may have been preceded by years of financial strain due to medical bills—or this may have been a woman's fourth miscarriage of a late-term baby—and to have someone *increase* those financial burdens is morally and spiritually wrong.

One widow stated starkly, "I never knew there was so much paper work, red tape, and decisions to be made in the *whole* world!"

I suppose the hardest adjustment in our talking with a mortician and discussing the funeral is the multitudinous amount of decisions that *must* be made. They are made, unfortunately, when we are at our lowest ebb emotionally.

Stephanie, the young widow who talked with me about her husband's death, said, "The only thing that helped me with all those funeral arrangements was that John and I had discussed what we would want if either of us died."

When I asked her what she would say to other young couples about the lessons of grief, she said, "Oh, early in their marriage the couple should discuss their future, including the possibility of death. They should be well-read up on death and dying."

Then she shared how much her chance reading about autopsy in the *Reader's Digest* had prepared her to immediately say yes about her husband's autopsy. "It was much easier to sign those papers after knowing about the importance of autopsies," she said.

Stephanie clearly heard her own song of mourning and in the beautiful memorial bulletin for her husband's service, she wrote these lines:

My Song

Praise to the Lord for
the difference He made
in John's life.

Praise to the Lord for
sparing him in length
of illness.

Praise to the Lord for
the family He chose John
to come from.

Praise to the Lord for
the friends we have.

Praise, praise to the Lord
for leading John to
marry me.

Praise to the Lord for
letting us choose our
eternal future.

"Even so, come, Lord Jesus."
Revelation 22:20 KJV

It was not the color or cost of John's casket, or the amount of money given to his memorial fund, but the proclamation of the radiant Christian message given at the service that turned his service into something very beautiful and touching.

My mother never discussed her funeral with me, but we had talked so many times of other services that I knew she wanted a victorious one—not one of sadness, but one of hope. She also wanted it in Dad's church—*not* at a mortuary. She wanted it to be in the place she'd served and worked, and she also wanted flowers, so we arranged it that way.

In my book *The Richest Lady in Town* I described the results of her memorial service when I wrote:

Breast cancer took everything from her except the sparkling spirit that fairly danced out of her dark brown eyes. In less than three years after her mastectomy and halfway through her fifty-seventh year, the Lord said, "That is *absolutely all* the pain I will allow her to bear," and He issued the command for Death to bring her to Him.

She went more than willingly, but we let her go with halting reluctance. We dressed her in her favorite flowered voile dress, surrounded her with a huge garden of flowers and packed in Dad's church with hundreds of people who listened to her funeral service.

John Gustafson's voice rang out in her favorite songs, "Until Then" and "My Heavenly Father Watches Over Me"; Chuck Leviton read a poem he had composed about her, "Marion Miller, the Quiet Fanatic."

Here is Chuck Leviton's poem:

> I'd call her a quiet fanatic,
>   One whose life had been changed,
> Who had come face to face with the Master
>   And since had not been the same.
>
> Yes, she was a quiet fanatic,
>   With consistency serving the King,
> She lived for a brighter tomorrow,
>   With heart full of faith she sang.
>
> She lived for a brighter tomorrow
>   While serving the King today,
> Her heart was in touch with the Master
>   And changes occurred when she prayed.

She was not a wide-eyed fanatic
Ranting and raving a creed,
But one of quiet dedication,
Reminding a world of its need.

She was a person of selfless denial,
Living a labor of love,
I'm talking of Marion Miller,
Whose heart had been touched from above.

She was a Christian of real compassion,
Whose power in prayer was alive,
Who tenderly loved the unlovely
Whose passion cannot be denied.

Thank God for Marion Miller,
Whose life was a blessing to all,
While life here has ceased for Marion,
Her blessings live on and on.

God used this quiet fanatic,
This vessel through which He flowed,
Lord, thank you for Marion Miller,
She was a privilege to know.

Dr. Ted Cole preached a stirring message about her life ending with "She is *not* dead." Then we all stood and sang "Great Is Thy Faithfulness" and watched as dear and precious people filed past us. We said our goodbys and tearfully watched as the casket lid was closed upon her.

My beloved friend, Dr. Samuel H. Sutherland, now president emeritus of Biola College, was one of those present at the funeral that hot September day. He didn't seem to mind the heat, but was so touched by the service he wrote Dr. Ted Cole, our pastor who officiated, these words:

Dear Dr. Ted,

I have participated in and heard many funeral messages, but I want to say that your remarks at the funeral of Mrs. Miller the other day were just about the most inspiring and most helpful I have ever heard. Everything you said was designed to encourage and uplift the loved ones and many friends of Mrs. Miller, who naturally were very sorrowful at the thought of their loss in her homegoing. I am sure it was a source

of great inspiration and untold comfort, especially to her loved ones.
The whole service was one of joy and triumph. Surely the sting of death
had been completely removed in the minds and hearts of all in attendance.

I had the privilege of meeting Mrs. Miller only once or twice, but she
must have been a wonderful person and devoted servant of our Lord,
because of the influence she had in the life of her beloved husband
and the wonderful product that she raised up in the person of our lovely
Joyce. Her loved ones, with one accord, rise up and call her blessed.

Again, let me thank you for the inspiration of that hour.

As I read Dr. Sutherland's words, especially "the inspiration of
that hour," I thought about the beauty of that day and in all that
happened at that funeral. The song was definitely one of mourning,
but with words like "Great Is Thy Faithfulness" ringing in our ears
we could not be totally bogged down in sadness.

The day after my mother's funeral most people went about their
own business, in their own world, and concerned with their own
affairs. That's as it should be, but what I was not prepared for was
"the day-after blues."

Now the real business of getting on with life had to begin again.
But like everyone who has ever faced the day-after-day-after-day-
after blues knows, it is no easy, pick-it-up-quickly accomplishment.

First of all, as I've previously stated, most Christians remember
to pray for the grieving family for only about two to three weeks.
Within a month the bereaved feel strangely alone.

I found myself staring out my sliding glass doors a month after
my mother died—overwhelmed with grief. "What is the matter with
me?" I wondered.

I grabbed a pen and wrote down:

Lord, why is it true that always in these moments,
These quiet times and places
I think of them?
Those I have tearfully returned to You.
I think, this morning, I shall die without them.
I'd love to answer the phone and hear her say,
"Hi darling daughter, what's the Lord done for you today?"

Oh, I know she's with You and very much alive,
But that's just the main point of my problem, Lord.
She's with You . . . and not here with me.

Or what about our son?
If he had stayed with us I might be taking him to nursery school,
Or picking up a fun assortment of his toys,
Or baking his favorite cookies.

Even KNOWING that You treat them tenderly doesn't help much.
I miss them all.
Sometimes I wish You'd hurry and come back so there could be
An end to these quiet times and places.

Your sweet, gifted Psalmist lost his son, too . . . .
Yet he spoke of being still and knowing You are God.
Was his heart shredding like mine in lonely grief?
Maybe in his quiet place that was the real message.

When I am still and
Knowing You
I am close to them.
Perhaps that's why I am filled with thoughts of them.

Thank you for pivoting my heart from lonely longings to
Your peace,
Your comfort and even a momentary measure of Your joy.

Yet—at these quiet times—
And places
I ache to see them and
I do not understand why I feel so alone
And am grieving so—

Why did I grieve so? Didn't I know my loved ones were with
the Lord? Didn't I know Grandpa was there—probably bouncing
our little David on his knee? Didn't I know Mother was proudly
showing off her grandson? Didn't I know they were all safe—happy
and with the Lord?

Yes—I suppose I did, but that business of being made in two
parts that C. S. Lewis wrote of was becoming a reality. I responded
with my God-side to where they were, what they were doing, and
who they were with, but I could not cope with my human side. The
loneliness closed in on me like a dreadful, gray fog.

Many bereaved have confirmed this experience for me. My
friend, Ann, told of the hundreds of people who prayed and sus-

tained her and her husband during the first weeks after the tragic death of their thirteen-year-old son. She said, "But as we felt and experienced the prayers of all those people in the first week of our son's death—we just as surely knew when they all *stopped* praying some weeks later."

It seems when the initial paralyzing shock begins to wear off, the bereaved slowly returns to consciousness like a person coming out of a deep coma. Senses and feelings return gradually, but mingled in with the good vibrations of being alive and alert again is the frightening pain of reality. It is precisely at this time when friends, assuming the bereaved is doing just fine, stop praying, stop calling, and stop doing all those little kind things that help so much.

We need to reverse this trend. In fact we must hold the bereaved person up to the Lord more during the first two years of grief than in the first two weeks.

Friends

O precious friends, who hold me up
In prayer, I could not drain my cup,
I could not walk this thorny road
Did you not plead for me to God!

How sweet and strange this gift of prayer!
You know my need and voice my care
And speak for me before His throne;
He reaches down, that Holy One,

To smooth the road before my feet;
And thus the circle is complete!
Dear friends of mine, I never knew
That I would owe so much to you!

MARTHA SNELL NICHOLSON

The song of grief will consume at least two years of our life to be sung. It seems that two birthdays, two Christmas holidays, and two family vacations have to pass before we begin to adjust to the empty place at the table or the now empty room at the end of the hall. And as the poem goes:

Dear friends of mine, I never knew
That I would owe so much to you!

When Carol's and Pete's seventeen-year-old son, Mike, was killed in a car accident, I made a personal commitment to pray for them and their family for at least one year.

The first year has just passed, this month, and today I received this revealing and remarkable letter from Carol.

Dear Joyce,

Thanks so much for remembering us with the lovely card and then for your faithfulness in prayer for me and my family this past year.

I know it was those prayers that made the difference between something to be only endured or something we and others could learn from. When you are overcome with grief there is a danger of depression, bitterness or even disillusion with God to creep in. I felt these thoughts and emotions at the door. But they never got in and took hold, because of the power of God there.

Instead there is a new appreciation of what the Resurrection Power really means. That same power that will raise Mike's lifeless body dwells in me now to keep me going. There is a new longing for my Heavenly Home. And there is a new concern for the use of the time given us on earth.

Most psychologists call this one-to-two-year period the time when "grief work" is accomplished. The song of grief, then, is important to hear and understand if the bereaved are ever to pick up the pieces of their lives and go on living.

The song of grief's work seems to be written in three parts:

1. At first there is that all-shattering, all-devastating shock that comes with death knowledge or news.
2. Then this is followed, a month or so later, by intense suffering and heightened loneliness.
3. Finally, at some point during the first year or second year, a slow, gradual healing of the mind, soul, and inner emotions begins to take place.

While it's difficult to listen to grief's music, we desperately need its healing work in our lives. Here are some of the reasons for listening closely to the lyrics and melody of grief's work song.

1. *We need the tears of grief.*

Following the shock of death knowledge come the greatest tensions in the world. To keep our tears locked up in some dark, inner corner is to suppress our grief and this can only lead to our emotions blowing up in our faces at a later date.

A woman whose thirteen-year-old daughter died suddenly of a brain hemorrhage went to the girl's funeral smiling. Everyone thought it was so wonderful because she was taking it all so well. "She never cried a single tear," they said of her, and I worried. My fears for her mental health were justified because about six months later she suffered a complete mental breakdown and to this date is still hospitalized.

We must not be ashamed of our tears. Jesus wept on hearing of his friend Lazarus's death (even though He knew He was about to give Lazarus a remission from death!). To weep is not to be guilty of a lack of faith, nor is it a sign of hopelessness. Crying is a natural part of the grieving process.

A widow who was the main speaker for a women's retreat recently, spoke of having *no* problems with grief or tears. She told how God was an all-purpose God and so she did *not* grieve *or* weep.

The widows in her audience listened in stunned agony. Their reaction was twofold and united: they were hurt and angry. They all wanted to ask:

"Why didn't God do that for me?"

"How come I cry and come unglued so easily?"

"Am I committing some sin or am I lacking in faith so God didn't take away *my* tears?"

"Did God do a special act of loving grace for her—and if so—why?"

I do not doubt the speaker was sincere and I'm sure she was truthful when she said she did not shed any tears—but she missed the beautiful melody the song of tears would have brought to her.

There are two verses in Revelation (7:17 and 21:4) that talk about God wiping away our tears. However, both verses refer to God and us being in *heaven* when this happens and *not* here on earth; and since we know there will be no tears in heaven, then the tears God wipes away *must* be the ones we shed on earth—*now!*

The Bible also clearly says we must weep with those who weep

(Romans 12:15). The value of tears and, yes, the weeping with those who weep, is beautifully described in the following letter by Mr. and Mrs. Walter Buster. Notice how many times they were comforted by the ministry of tears at the death of their three-and-one-half-year-old son. It was printed in the newsletter of the First Baptist Church of Fullerton, California.

A Letter to the Church Family

Our Dear Friends:

We thank you for being real with emotions; no one can be strong about death. There is a special language for moments like these. However, it can't be written. It is expressed only through embraces, tears, and compassion of loving people.

Our beautiful child died, and we don't understand why. We ached, bled, and wept. We hurt so that survival seemed impossible. The awful depression numbed our bodies, and our thoughts screamed out-of-control that it was all an ugly dream.

If we had been asked off-the-cuff before the tragedy in one of those meaningless philosophical discussions that now seem so empty, we might have chosen solitude for a time like Thursday evening. *BUT PEOPLE CAME.* There were no meaningless words—only broken hearts, embraces, and love. Our hearts were broken and so were those of our precious friends.

On Thursday night we learned the value of intruding upon the hurting. We were not left alone in our grief. People with wet faces and eager, grabbing hearts broke down the facades we had created and gave their love.

The small groups of which we had been a part saved Sue and me. The groups of friends with whom we met to pray and share were like our own torn flesh. Because we had shared so much before, they immediately reached and took those chances we always have a hard time taking (total involvement). They touched our faces, embraced and held our weary bodies, and shared our wounded souls.

But, compassion has no age. A group of young people came to us. Young people with whom Sue and I had laughed, cried, and loved. This time *we needed them.* They had not been taught to share in the agony of death. They were really afraid to come. But, they did come. And, they held us and wept with us. We were overcome by their love and compassion. They loved, shared, wept *unashamedly.*

But, the group grew larger. The walls of an institution we had worked to change, fell. People reached, reached, reached, and, we needed and wanted them. Each person that came was ripped and angered and crushed with us. We felt it!

Christ's love came in all those people who pushed us back into the terrible reality, and bandaged us with hope and love. We love you all.

And you, our dear friends, Emory and Loeta [the pastor and his wife]. You gave us new life when we wanted only death. You gave hope and life and the reality of going on. How do you do it? God gave you a gift that others need so deeply. You are so tender and loving. I told Sue you were *exact*. You did and said the perfect things. How can we ever, ever thank you? The service was just as we wanted it with favorite memories of our son and our hope. Oh God, how we loved our little Joel. The hurt will never really stop. But you, the tender people of our church, helped so much.

We're moving to a new city. We're not running away. Our plans had been made before, and we feel it best to carry them out now. Come see us. Invite us to your homes. Don't hesitate to share with us your memories of Joel. They are so precious to us, and how we appreciate those of you who took time to care for, share, and love our little guy.

How can we thank each of you for your love? It has simply seen us through this time. *Please know this.* One thing we have surely learned is that "words of comfort" are nonexistent. No one has magic words. Yet there is a comfort through your clasping, embracing, and sobbing with us. We can't adequately thank you for coming to our homes, and to Joel's memorial service. For we have learned above all things that God's love comes through people.

Love,

WALT & SUE BUSTER and all our family
who were overwhelmed by your love.

This letter was followed by a beautiful statement from the pastor, the Reverend Emory C. Campbell. It said:

The foregoing letter from Walt and Sue Buster expresses beautifully what the church really is about. When I received word on Thursday night of the tragic death of little Joel Buster I was at Thousand Pines with our Jr. High Camp. By the time I drove down the mountain, our church family had surrounded them with love. It is so good that God has given us the capacity to cry when we hurt and to cry with others when they hurt.

Of the church St. Paul said truly, "If one part suffers, all parts suffer with it." We are one in the Spirit and thus we feel deeply with each other.

Love and joy to you all,

EMORY C. CAMPBELL

"The capacity to cry when we hurt and to cry with others when they hurt," says it right where it's at! We must develop the capacity to cry. I know a marvelous minister who was aware of this need in his life and prayed for "the ministry of tears" to be developed in his own heart. God answered his prayer and his overall ministry has new depth and dimension to it.

In time of bereavement we need tears to wash away the gray tensions of our soul and when we do cry it does *not* require an apology *or* an explanation.

Also with our tears we need to reach out, grasp (even briefly), and to physically embrace the bereaved. In the preceding letter the line, "They touched our faces, embraced and held our weary bodies and shared our wounded souls," tells in an unprecedented way of the exceptional value of combining tears of understanding with tender, wordless embraces. I feel weeping with each other is best done while holding the hands of the brokenhearted. We worry about what we will *say* to the bereaved when a handclasp, a quick hug, or a small touch on the shoulder says it all mutely, but magnificently best.

2. *We need the slowness of grief.*

Time feels like it has come to a complete stop after we lose a loved one. The most unbearable stretch of the day seems to be in those dark hours just before daybreak. It's so cold, so dark, and so forbidding that time of the day, our anxiety gets thick enough to cut with a knife.

However, do not be impatient with the slowness of grief's music. Its *largo* tempo (which plods along at a maddening slow pace) may be very essential for a healthy recovery. We long for the upbeat tempo of what we recognize as "normal" for our life's melody, but it may take a very long time to finally play out grief's song.

Since our baby was the first of anyone close to us to die, I had no idea working through the grief would go so slowly.

One afternoon I blurted out to a friend, "I don't understand why

I'm still crying or why this hurts so much—after all, it's been two whole weeks since David died."

Months later I was even more impatient with myself. I reasoned I was being very immature over all of this and somehow I felt grieving (or crying) was a sign of weakness. The idea that I might be right on schedule for a very normal timetable never occurred to me.

If we rush this time of adjusting along too fast, we rob grief of the work of the gradual healing it must carry out. We must not be in such a hurry to get ourselves or our bereaved friends "back to normal." It is essential to remember "normal" has been forever altered into abnormal. We do the bereaved an injustice when we do not allow them to grieve. And since we need to grieve, if we are not allowed to, *we* create yet another problem: *guilt*. The bereaved do not want to walk away from a grave site and bring down a mental curtain, shutting off forever the person who has died. That is cruel and somehow seems to be a very unloyal thing to do. This causes the guilty feeling in the bereaved of not being true or faithful to the deceased. They must be encouraged to talk, express their feelings—whether they be sad, angry, or lonely—and take all the time they need. The natural slowness of grief cooperates here and can be a useful tool toward adjustments in living.

When I experienced my losses, I desperately wanted to talk with someone about death and dying. Instead, I was given some rather sticky-sweet, pie-in-the-sky-by-and-by books that depressed me even more than I already was. What I needed (at that point) was not books, but people.

The books told me I should not be sad at losing my loved one because I was a Christian with hope. But what I didn't understand was—if that were true about my Christianity and hope—how come I *was* sad—fantastically *sad?*

What I needed to know was that grief and sadness would be with me for a while. It would have helped had I known that the slowness of grief and the passing of time would give me the perfect opportunity to express my sorrow and begin healing.

Eventually I'd emotionally heal and see the lovely hope of God, but at that point in my grieving to hear or read, "Buck up, life isn't quite all *that* bad!" was a frustration quite beyond comprehension.

If you have just lost your husband, wife, child or friend, recognize and understand the work of the slowness of grief and I know some of the fear and dread of this time will dissipate. It will help, too, if you commit to memory this verse from John: "No, I will not abandon you or leave you as orphans in the storm—I will come to you" (John 14:18 LB).

If, just before dawn, when the hours are at their darkest, you repeat those beautifully honest and true words, the tempo of grief will not seem so slow. You will be better able to wait it out.

3. *We need to accept the apathy of grief.*

For someone who has always been a "bundle of energy" or "full of pep and vinegar" the apathy of grief is an arduous, toilsome frustration to grasp mentally. It is difficult to decipher the change in our regular, basic, routine methods and attitudes.

The apathy of grief strikes a normally decisive person and instantly one finds it takes a superhuman amount of effort to make even the smallest decision.

A woman discovers in the first few months of her widowhood she does not have the strength, will, or remotest desire at 5:30 P.M. to choose between mashed potatoes or baked potatoes. It all seems so useless to decide on *anything.*

C. S. Lewis describes this apathy as the "laziness of grief."

I saw a vivid example of the apathy or "laziness" of grief a month or two after my mother died.

I had driven over to my father's home to visit him and I was appalled at the messiness and utter chaos of his house. He and my sister were the only two people living there, yet the house looked as if several families were existing there—all crowded in together.

It was when I started to clean the house up and to put it into some semblance of order that I discovered the main core and reason for the mess. It was all the opened mail.

Evidently my father had received even more mail than usual each day, opened it where he happened to be, read it, and then laid it down wherever he had been standing.

There were stacks of mail in the usual place in the kitchen, on the desk; but also on the stove, the refrigerator, and on top of the washer. Mail and sympathy cards were stuck in between the wooden dowels of room dividers; they were all over the bedrooms and the den; and there was not a table, chair, or couch in the living room without some cards or bits and pieces of mail. Even the bathroom did not escape its landslide of litter.

My father had lost his wife of thirty-seven years and he had also lost all interest in going on. His curiosity about the contents of the mail helped him to open it, but the apathy of grief had so stolen his drive and zest for living that he simply laid it down wherever he was, without responding in any way.

We must realize that when death hits us it will completely disrupt our entire life schedule. "Oh, what's the use?" will be our most continual thought. But apathy, like the slowness of grief, is only temporary. After the first anguishing shock of death has subsided a bit, the bereaved will need special attention, love, and support because this period of apathy is so subtle they do not notice it happening. They may not be aware of it at all.

This is the moment for friends *not* to ask, "Is there anything I can do?" but, rather, it is a time for friends to be alert and sensitive to the work apathy is trying to achieve. When the bereaved is ready to resume normal social functions, family relationships, or daily employment, friends can help the transition by doing, not asking.

My journal, written soon after David died, tells about my adjustment to the apathetic period of time in my own grief:

In the past months of pregnancy, I've never been so ill. Now I am recovering from both that illness and David's death. Everytime I turn around I hear someone say, "If there's anything I can do, just let me know." I just smile and say, "No, thank you." Actually there's much to be done, but somehow I simply don't want to do anything and wouldn't dream of asking anyone else to.

During that time a few of my friends *did* come to the rescue. They understood, somehow, about my apathy and they didn't ask about helping—they just did! There was the college girl, Andrea, home for Christmas, who said, "When you want the children out of the house for a while, I'll pick them up," or the other college girl, Glenda, who said, "It's the day before Christmas and I'm free. Which do you want me to do, the dusting or the ironing?" (She ironed.) Or Eleanor, who called and said, "I'm fixing dinner for your family one night this week—which night would be best?" Or the friend who simply shoved a cake into Laurie's hands at the front door and said, "Tell your mother this is from Shirley." Or Dorothy, our minister's wife, one of the busiest women I know, who called and said, "I've just baked two lemon pies, would it be convenient for me to bring them over now?" Or Al Sanders, a business executive, who said, "On Monday I'm sending my personal secretary over for the day to help you take care of your mail." (His wife sent a roast, too!)

Jane Huff, in her book *Whom the Lord Loveth* said that after a long illness of hers, she KNEW what to do for people in need! A friend asked her what the first thing would be—like for a sick person. Jane's answer was, "The dishes!"

The bereaved need to be surrounded by such friends who "do the dishes" and whose actions are motivated by Paul's words in Ephesians 5:15–17:

> So be careful how you act; these are difficult days. Don't be fools; be wise: make the most of every opportunity you have for doing good. Don't act thoughtlessly, but try to find out and do whatever the Lord wants you to.

The secret is in asking the Lord what you can do as a friend—and then doing it in His name to help during this temporary lull in a grieving person's life-style.

4. *We need to know the humility of grief.*

The intense pain of grief has a unique way of leveling our pride and produces a humility which enlarges our growth of character. The music of this portion of grief's song is not too pleasant or soothing, but then real growth is not too soothing, either, when it's happening. It is painful to grow. I wish that were not true, but it seems any experience which forces us into growth will be accompanied by its own costly expense and pain-filled agony.

As a child, growing up for me was physically quite an ordeal! I generally managed to catch every germ and disease that came along. Most of the time my constant companions were flu, colds, and bronchitis. However, those years of being ill developed some very special resources in me. For instance, because of those years, I have learned how to be alone without being lonely. I also learned how to fill up time while being confined; in fact, that's where I found out about reading books. So many illnesses gave me an empathy for the sick and my capacity to care took shape under the humbling experiences of being sick.

Today when I hear someone brag, "I've never been sick a day in my whole life," I feel a little sorry for them because pain and illness produce a quality of aliveness within our souls like nothing else can do.

That braggadocious statement also tells me that when they *do* get sick, as they probably will, they will have a difficult time coping and adjusting to the pain and depression of illness.

God will have to do a special work of grace and mercy in their hearts or their pride and patience may not hold out!

My pastor, Dr. Ted Cole, told of the work of humility within the framework of grief as he observed it in his father, Rolland Cole. His father—a strong, healthy, robust, six-foot-four-inch-tall man, weighing 250 pounds—had little sickness or physical problems in life. There was not too much he couldn't handle. Then, in his sixties, cancer moved in and began to take over. As dying became imminent, Dr. Ted watched, with incredible fascination, his dad's character transformation. The father, once ready to impatiently denounce people or events in a critical way, began to develop large amounts of Christian love and patience. The sicker he became and the closer dying advanced toward him, the more his pride was leveled and humility—beautiful, gracious, patient humility—took over.

We must learn the value of grief's lessons and not be too hard on the dying or the bereaved while they are grieving. We must not be critical of their actions for we do not know how we will react when sickness and death make us their target.

5. *We need to use grief as a creative gift.*

As much as we need the tears, the slowness, the apathy, and the humility of grief, we must not stay there for the rest of our lives. We should give those elements enough time to do the real work of grief in our lives and then consider our loss in terms of a creative gift.

The famous Tracy Clinic for deaf children was never thought, dreamed, or even considered until Spencer Tracy and his wife gave birth to a totally deaf son. Out of little John's deafness, this clinic, one of the finest in the world, was developed and brought into existence.

In the terrible months of grieving solitude following my mother's death, I never dreamed I'd find anything creative in dying. But, as I wrote in *The Richest Lady in Town:*

It should have been the end of her, but then we found all her note-books: big spiral ones, little spiral ones, date books, secretary pads, loose-leaf binders, and even her diary kept before she met my father. They were a treasure house of ideas, theories, and inspiration—the essence of fifty-seven years of being God's woman.

Over and over again I read and reread those books she left. It was the most creative collection of gifts I've ever seen and it came straight from God. I've used her material in every book I've written so far and how grateful I am that while she was alive she took the time to write down her thoughts, ideas, and prayers. She had no plans for publishing, yet she is now published. Those notebooks are far more important to me in value than any financial inheritance of *any* amount I could have received.

Another person to use her personal grief as a creative gift to help others has been Dale Evans Rogers. It was because Dale and Roy Rogers lost their precious two-year-old daughter, Robin, that the society's attitude and treatment of mongoloid children has drasti-cally changed. Dale took her grief and poured herself into the book *Angel Unaware.*

Because she was willing to be honest and use her grief as a creative gift, Dale threw open the doors of thousands of homes. Families who had previously hidden their mongoloid children in the dark shadows of their private lives, came forward and began to accept God's gentle healing. *Mongoloid* was no longer treated as a word to be avoided at all cost after Dale's beautifully shared story.

Dr. Norman Vincent Peale wrote of Dale in *Angel Unaware:*

She is a mother who has won great victory over great sorrow . . . . I saw at once that Robin, her baby, had not lived and died in vain. Where most babies die and leave the mother crushed, Robin put on immortality and her mother found the very joy of God in what might otherwise have been an overwhelming tragedy.

That book was only the beginning of Dale using grief as a creative gift. In the twenty years that have followed the publication of Robin's story, Dale has lost several children, and the rich store of books that have flowed out of her pen have become a scintillating ministry to millions of people.

In my own losses, Dale's books always reached me at precisely the exact moment they were needed.

Soon after our infant son died, Dale's daughter, Debbie, was killed in a tragic bus accident. Dale, using her grief as a gift, penned the book *Dearest Debbie.*

My mother gave it to me the day the first copy reached California and it came none too soon.

Our children, Rick and Laurie, were having a very hard time adjusting to their brother David's dying—just when God had promised they'd have a *healthy* brother. I sat our children down and, out loud, I read the entire book about Debbie. When I finished I said, "Now children, what did that book say to you?" Both children were crying. Rick was twelve and Laurie ten, but Laurie voiced their identical feelings out loud for me when she tearfully said, "'That book helps me to understand about David dying and I feel better about him being with God, but don't read it again to me because it's beautiful-sad." The healing had begun and it was motivated by Dale's willingness to accept grief as a creative gift to give others.

If we will look into, examine, and put into practice these five definite works: the tears, slowness, apathy, humility, and creativity of grief—the harshness of the mourning song softens, fades, and then sweeps back with its own *newborn,* majestic splendor. We can never be the same again and we *can* bear to listen to the song without breaking apart.

9

The Lasting Song of Restoration

. . . out of His infinite riches in Jesus
He giveth and giveth and giveth again.
ANNIE JOHNSON FLINT

The work of restoration must happen in our lives after death has taken a loved one away or we may never recover from our loss. We may never pick up the pieces or ever feel whole again.

It is no wonder then, at so many funerals, we hear the Twenty-Third Psalm. If it's not repeated by the minister, rabbi, or priest, it is printed for us to read or its message is brought to us in song, but somehow we are made aware of the poetic beauty of this oft-quoted psalm. Its lyrical prose seems to transcend all racial boundaries and all religious creeds and it is powerful even when the deceased is *not* a Christian.

The reason for its enormous popularity down through the years is its fantastic success in helping to restore our splintered, fractured emotions.

To me the key word is found early in the psalm in the third verse. Here are some translations:

"He restoreth my soul" (KJV).

"He revives my soul" (MLB).

"He restores my failing health" (LB).

"He restores my soul" (RSV).

All that third verse says basically is:

1. God
2. Heals
3. Me

and it turns out to be the most important message of our life. There we are: alone, sometimes cut in half, weary, and heartsick, when we hear the music of restoration start up with the lyrics:

"Because the Lord is my Shepherd, I have everything I need!"

"He lets me rest in the meadow grass and leads me beside the quiet streams—"

Later, we hear:

"Even when walking through the dark valley of death I will not be afraid, for you are close beside me, guarding, guiding all the way."

As a Christian, God's ability to bring the lasting, continuous song of restoration to my being is just one of the exciting fringe benefits of really knowing Christ.

But what of those who do not know Christ? What good do the magnificent words of the Twenty-Third Psalm do except to pour a little oil on a large, gaping, bleeding wound? What about those bereaved souls who can only guess there *may* be a life after death —or those who "hope" the person who died has gone to a heaven (if there is one)?

I remember the first time I observed people with no hope at a funeral. They had no chance of restoration's song restoring their lives.

They had stumbled into the service on time, but in an alcoholic stupor. I reacted to their being very drunk in a superspiritual (absolutely nauseating) way. "How dare they?" I wondered. Angrily, I silently denounced their actions as definitely in bad taste.

With one destructive blow to my superspiritual pride, God's words cut and leveled me off right at my ankles.

Joyce, why are you so filled with righteous indignation? Why are you so quick to criticize their behavior? Don't you realize they are sorrowing with no hope? They do not know Me, they do not know I've come to give eternal life, they do not know that there is more and they think this is all there is. You must not be angry with them because they have escaped death's ugly reality by drinking. What else do they have to turn to?

I looked again, this time with a softened heart, at the rather drunk, grieving family of the man in the casket. Even though my compassion was newly acquired, I could clearly see that people without faith, without forgiveness, and without God's peace come to funerals to say good-bye. They do not come to whisper, "I'll see you in the morning." Death comes to them as the finale, the last farewell, the killing blow; and certainly no psalm, even the twenty-third, is going to put things right again. It is easier for them to bear the funeral if their senses are not exposed to the raw, naked hurt of death, so they come in an attitude of numb denial—hardly seeing, hearing, or feeling.

What a difference for the person who comes to Christ, asks Him to forgive his sins, and invites the Lord God into his total life! Living not only completely changes, but so does—*forever*—death and dying! It's a new ball game altogether for Christians. We are not left hopeless, we are not left with *only* these brief days on earth, but, fantastically, we have gained eternity. We do not have to vaguely fantasize about the possibility of reincarnation, or whether or not there *is* life after death—we *know* the positive answers to death's past and future. So when we do sorrow it is this hope of God that will not let us sorrow in terms of *finality* and *defeat*. We are not abandoned to the lonely struggle of living out our frustrating grief alone. In short, our hope in Christ and living after death with Him *is* our restoration.

Paul never said it better and he never said it clearer than when he wrote to the church at Thessalonica:

And now, dear brothers, I want you to know what happens to a Christian when he dies so that when it happens, you will not be full of sorrow, as those are who have no hope. For since we believe that Jesus died and then came back to life again, we can also believe that when Jesus returns, God will bring back with him all the Christians who have died.

1 Thessalonians 4:13, 14

Every time I've seen those two verses lately I think of Mary Ann, a lady who belonged to our church. After her death her husband, sorrowing, yes, but not without hope, wrote this letter to their Sunday-school class. He ended the letter with those marvelous words of Paul.

Dear Chapel Class Friends:
These flowers are in a small way in appreciation for your Christian love and kindness and gifts of food for me and my family during a time of life's greatest sorrow—to lose a lovely wife and Mother.
Mary Ann loved each of you and was heartbroken when she could no longer attend class due to her poor health. She was so thrilled with the special recording of the class music and message, that she had me play it over and over for her. We thank you from the bottom of our hearts for the love and joy you brought to her in this manner.
Please be comforted in knowing that Mary Ann believed in the Saving Blood of Jesus Christ, and that she prayed for the Members of the Chapel Class at each opportunity, asking God's richest blessings upon each of you. She prayed also that the Lord Jesus Christ would take her home to be with Him, for she believed to be absent from the body is to be present with the Lord in Heaven.
Although we shall grieve the loss of Mary Ann, and there will be a great void in our lives, we are comforted by God's Holy Word when we read 1 Thessalonians 4:13–18.

Yours in Christian Love—
BOB EDWARDS

When God wanted to restore my heart with His hope, He let me find my mother's very explicit explanation of the hope we have in God. Among her papers I found the penciled copy of the letter she wrote to a dear friend about six months before her death. Here, set down so accurately, is the picture of death, when it comes to Christians. She wrote:

My dear Esther,

In the recent death of your dear mother these few lines of encouragement are easy to write to you because you have had the experience of rebirth and you belong to the Kingdom of God. You know, in a vital, personal way that you are one of God's little children and you also know that this human existence is but the first act to our spiritual (real) existence.

Belief in Christ and *His* immortality gives us the moral strength and the guidance we need for virtually every action in our daily lives. When you came in contact with Christ you received *eternal* life. The Word of God teaches us—and strengthens our belief in the continuity of our spiritual existence after death.

We live for a very short time in our natural bodies, but we live *eternally* in our spiritual bodies. So the passing or, plainly spoken, the death of your dear mother is in reality a continuation of her existence in what is now her spiritual body. Her human body died. That body was no longer strong enough or well enough for her to use it any more. But Esther, your *mother* did not die—only her body did! St. Paul says, as there's a natural body, so will there be a spiritual body.

It is wonderful to know (and believe) that we shall know one another just as we know our loved ones here on earth.

I know you have had a terrible loss and heartache. The breaking of human ties and the closing of earthly chapters in our lives brings sorrow and pain, but healing comes to us when we accept the reality of death and dying. Healing comes, too, when we realize that our life continues in another form *more* glorious than the human mind can imagine!

In trying to sort all this grief and troubled times out in your life, let us admit frankly that we are entering a realm of faith. Since no one has returned to tell us what lies on the other side, we must go on living by faith. Faith in the existence of God and faith by the teachings of Jesus Christ.

Death, then, is not merely a solemn, dark curtain, rung down on the first act on the stage of this all too brief earthly life, but it *is* the lifting of the curtain on the most wonderful and final act of life's drama. We are passed from death unto life!

Your life, dear Esther, is a blessing to many so may this recent experience show that life's greatest achievement, in the long run, is to know and have peace with God.

My prayer is for God to give you strength for your *immediate* needs.

In the bond of Christian love,

MARION

My mother had no way of knowing (unless God whispered it to her) that I would find that letter almost a year after her death and be restored by reading it. She also couldn't have known that wherever she had used the name Esther I had inserted "Joyce" and it had brought a large measure of healing to my heart. I was able to see the work of restoration beginning to happen in my life.

As nearly as I can put it together, God does His remarkable work of restoration by three methods. I have, in these last pages, put them down for you. It is my hope—no, my prayer—that God will open your mind, your emotions, and your will to receive *His* restoration. The last thing in the world I want to do is smugly pat you on the back and tell you "everything is coming up roses" or parrot the phrase, "Isn't it nice they (the dead) are with the Lord?" I do not want to be sticky-sweet with a bunch of clichés, pat answers, or unreal phrases. But *God does restore our souls and we can recuperate* from our devastating losses if we are wise enough to hear the inspiring melody of God's mourning song.

Listen, then, to the first faint strains of restoration's song as it begins with one word.

1. *Forgiveness!*   •

Nothing can be done for us in our grief—whether we are grieving for ourself and our own impending death or for someone else's death—unless we begin with forgiveness.

For the Christian involved in death or dying, forgiveness starts with forgiving (of all people) God!

We will have our time of angrily demanding of God the whys of our problem as my mother did when she gave the Lord a verbal tongue-lashing over Dr. Carlson's death; but healing, hope, and acceptance of death will not come until we forgive God for allowing death to happen.

I spoke at a luncheon this week and a woman heard my brief remarks about this book as I shared some of the lessons I'd learned about death. At the close of the luncheon, while she did not know I'd be writing about forgiveness, she felt led of God to share a personal word or two with me. I'm grateful because she told me of losing her darling, beloved grandson and of her inner reactions that followed. She said there was no way she could accept the little boy's death. She felt angry toward God and could not come up with any reasonable explanation as to why this child had died. The more she thought about it, the madder she got; and one day, as loud and clear as a human voice would sound, she heard the Lord say, *Will you forgive Me for his death?* She said her first reaction was to be stunned by the news that God was *asking* her for forgiveness. Next she realized she had been accusing and blaming God for the death. As soon as she answered the Lord's question with a yes, the peace of God gently slipped into the vacant spot of her heart and she was healed.

In a letter to my brother Cliff, just a few months before she died, my mother positively documented the fact that she had forgiven God for His direction and handling in her life's course. She wrote:

I thank God for the joy and peace I have in my heart made possible by Him.

Tomorrow I go to U.C.L.A. again, but I am not afraid and I thank God that Christ is with me.

My son, God has a chartered course for all of us. He whispered so sweetly to me a few weeks ago that if I put Him first in my life—He'll see that I come in second.

So I put myself in His care. Now I've asked Him to pilot the course laid out for me and for my dear family.

God bless you, Son—you will face hard, trying days—but I know you'll come through with flying colors.

Be not afraid neither be dismayed for the Lord God is with you wherever you go.

Lovingly,
MOTHER

She wanted my brother (and all of us) to know she had forgiven God for the "chartered course" He'd obviously begun plotting for her. That is exactly why she started the letter with thanks to God. Then she made sure that we knew of her conversation with the Lord so we'd know it was all right between them.

I think she also wanted us to know that even when we didn't *see* any evidences of God caring or working in our lives, we were to take the barest amount of faith we had and *remember* God's loving promises.

She ended with the added admonition to not only remember God's promises, but to remember them *without* fear—no matter how trying the days might become.

That my mother had forgiven God for cancer and her impending death was known not only by us in the family, but by friends as well.

A letter from Jeanne, a dear friend of ours, after my mother's death reads, in part:

About your mother's death, my mind did a flashback of two scenes.

One—The first time I met your parents at the little old musty smelling synagogue in Reseda where your dad started his little church and from which I went representing them as their first missionary to a foreign land. [They had no church building so Dad rented the synagogue on Sunday for their services until their sanctuary was built.]

Two—Then several years later as I stood with both your mom and dad, holding hands and forming a circle for prayer in their living room. Even though your mom was up, she was unable to go out anymore. Her prayer (I can *still* feel even though she was well aware of her condition) was beautiful and with her gentle words she melted my very soul. She drew us all nearer that day to the Christ she was soon to meet. That was the last time I saw her—here.

My mother's prayer that day would have never drawn Jeanne closer to the Lord had it not been for the song of forgiveness in Mother's heart.

My sister, Marilyn, who was fourteen at the time of Mother's death, had to forgive God, too. The start of restoration's song in Marilyn's heart began as I wrote of it in *The Richest Lady in Town:*

It was just hours after our mother's funeral. Marilyn was fourteen, frightened, and unbelievably hurt and bewildered by Mother's death.

Friends and relatives had left. I'd gone home with my family; my brother, Cliff, had taken a military jet back to Vietnam; and my father had wearily gone to bed.

She went into the den and, realizing her aloneness, asked God to be her Friend, Savior, and Comforter. In short, she did an incredible thing —*she forgave* the Lord for taking her mother. He, in turn, melted the hurt and bitterness and began to heal her torn heart. In those moments she started to become the beautiful, wealthy person we love.

When I think of her, at such a young age forgiving the Lord for Mother's death, I remember the widow who said angrily to me, "Just how am I supposed to be thankful for my husband's death two years ago?"

I told her she'd *never* get over that death until she could get to the bottom of the problem. There she stood, some two years after her husband's death, still shaking her fist in God's face demanding to know why He had done this terrible thing to her. She will always be spiritually poor until the lesson of forgiveness melts her hardened heart and begins its healing.

Marilyn is rich because her forgiveness is always up-to-date. She's determined to be the woman God wants her to be.

Besides forgiving God, we need to forgive ourselves, too. Very often in the days of grief following the loss of a loved one we pile up a huge stack of regrets. We remember each and every thing we did (or did not do) with the deceased and we relive old conflicts. We reconstruct everything we wish we had done and suffer deeply with those regrets and remorseful feelings.

Martha Snell Nicholson said it best when she wrote this poem:

Remembered Sin

I made a lash of my remembered sins.
I wove it firm and strong, with cruel tip,
And though my quivering flesh shrank from the scourge,
With steady arm I plied the ruthless whip.

For surely I, who had betrayed my Lord,
Must needs endure this sting of memory.
But though my stripes grew sore, there came no peace,
And so I looked again to Calvary.

His tender eyes beneath the crown of thorns
Met mine; His sweet voice said, "My child, although
Those oft-remembered sins of thine have been
Like crimson, scarlet, they are now like snow.

"My blood, shed here, has washed them all away,
And there remaineth not the least dark spot,
Nor any memory of them; and so
Should you remember sins which God forgot?"

I stood there trembling, bathed in light, though scarce
My tired heart dared to hope. His voice went on:
"Look at thy feet, My child." I looked, and lo,
The whip of my remembered sins was gone!

I'm sure God longs to take away our whips of remembered sins. But if those painful slashes on our souls are ever to heal, we need to forgive ourselves as God has forgiven us. We need to deliberately dwell on the important fact that when God *forgave* those sins and past regrets He *forgot* them as well.

After we have checked out our forgiveness and seen if it's updated to forgive God and self, then we may need to see if forgiveness is needed toward other people.

The healing that follows forgiveness in my own case came after I forgave God for the death of our son and then forgave (by God) my parents for their not attending David's funeral. I've already related that until I put my regrets and angers into God's hands I was sick, not only physically, but emotionally as well.

When we can lay the people, places, and events into the forgiving hands of God, we have taken a major step toward healthy, normal living once more. In fact, there is nothing we can do with the regretful people and events of yesterday except entrust them to the God of all tomorrows.

If the first strains of God's song of restoration begin with forgiveness, then you can rest assured the bridge part of the melody in the middle of the song will be acceptance.

2. *Acceptance.*

In learning about dying and transferring the lessons on to me, my mother lived the best, most profound moments of all her life. I will remember her for many years of delightful things, but I will remember her most for her *atttitude* of acceptance toward her own death during her last seven weeks.

I pray I will be able to teach the God-given attitudes of acceptance to my children even before it is time for me to keep my appointment with death. I have been working on it now for several years.

Fear and denial are at the opposite ends of the world from acceptance and I must realize this when I begin to teach my children about death and dying. I wish I had started out earlier with our children, but like every other parent in the world, I felt our children would know soon enough about death's dark curtain and I thought, "Why bring it up?"

But death is a vital part of living and preparation and discussion of this almost taboo subject will be valuable to them as they mature into adults.

Children should be included in before- and after-death conversation and they should be allowed to hear the funeral plans and decisions being made. It's not a time to hustle them outside or stop talking about "Grandma who just died" when they enter a room. To let them listen to our grief and see our tears is to let them know *their* grief is not abnormal. They are feeling sad, too, and to include them in our discussions and to answer their questions helps them to allow the work of mourning to be accomplished.

Recently on a TV special called "The Right to Die," Dr. Elisabeth Kübler-Ross stated that she felt children must be able to accept death and its processes at least by the time they are twenty years of age. She went on to state that if they had not come to grips with death acceptance by their twenties then it would be very hard on them later when they tried to cope with death.

A couple of years ago our family had quite a discussion about accepting death. We talked about the "what ifs" of dying.

What if Dad died?

What if Mom died?

What if you died? What would you want for your funeral?

And the conversation which started during dinner went on long after dinner was finished.

We will always remember the discussion. The reasons none of us will ever forget that night are twofold: (1) For some strange reason, we all waxed hysterically funny in the wit department, and (2) we made some serious statements that will be remembered and (some of them) carried out in the event of our deaths.

It was at that dinner I learned, for the first time, my husband did *not* want an open casket. ("If that lid is open I'm going to reach up during the middle of the service and pull it down over me! I don't want everybody staring down and saying, 'My, my, doesn't Dick look natural!'") Later on I found he wanted my dress (at his funeral) to be powder blue in color. (Rick said prophetically, "Well, I hope no one phones to console Mother after Dad's gone because she won't be home—she'll be out shopping for a blue dress.") We all agreed, that night, we would want a memorial service in our church rather than in a mortuary; and songs like "When Morning Gilds the Skies," "How Great Thou Art," and "Blessed Assurance" should be sung. My husband found I wanted flowers—tons of flowers—none of this, "In lieu of flowers, please send money to. . . ." I remembered at my mother's funeral, when I could bear to study her beloved face no more, my heart found refuge and great comfort in the hundreds of floral bouquets.

While we laughed and loved a great deal that night, we took some serious steps toward firming up acceptance of death as a part of living in all our hearts—not just our children's. We concluded that really the funeral should be a *Christian worship service to God in loving memory of the one who had died.*

Not only must we teach our children acceptance of the death process, but we must work with acceptance on our own part. Nothing facilitates this faster than making out a will.

Frankly, I never did think too much about our making out a will. I felt my husband and I (in our forties) were too young to bother with it, and to procrastinate seemed to be the best plan. Also, since I'll probably do my best to spend most of what is allotted to us financially in life, I really didn't think there would be too much left after we died to divide and conquer.

That was before I read a powerful message in Catherine Marshall's *To Live Again*, which was, "Peter . . . had left no will."

It was in those few printed pages that Catherine Marshall related the horror and agony she endured after her husband died, leaving no will. After reading it, my husband and I came to a point of decision: we would make out a will immediately. So we did!

Our education on what happens to "property and things" after death escalated considerably. We found that if, at the time of death, there is no written, valid will, the *state chooses* the beneficiaries of all *your* properties and the state's decisions are absolutely final!

We also found that many, many Christians (something like eight out of ten) do not write any will at all. Out of the few Christians who do make wills, almost 50 percent do *not* remember the Lord's work or their home church.

Some of the bereaved I've talked with have been stumbling down dark, discouraging corridors for years because no will was left. Any money they thought they had was used up in probate taxes, and went to state funds. Having no will produced one financial headache after another for them. Acceptance of death is next to impossible with these overwhelmingly disturbing financial burdens. To experience the agonies of settling an estate (even a very small one) is to experience frustrations of the greatest magnitude.

Should the day come when our children must decide what to do with our possessions, they will have a clear, concise, valid will to direct them. Also, we have left for them a Christian will—one which provides for them *and* the Lord's work.

After our children are taken care of, our will leaves a percentage of our "estate" to our church and to a couple of marvelous Christian organizations. That is one way to do it (by percentages); but our friend and business executive, Roark Moudy, has his will bequeathing cash monies to the Lord's work, and either way is fine!

The actual financial amount of our estate is not too fantastic, but the peace of mind for our children and the knowledge that our money will go to the Lord's work (and not someone else's) pushes us out of denial into healthy acceptance.

We encourage acceptance not only by freely discussing death and dying with our families and by making sure there is a valid will, but by one other important way as well: by understanding the five stages of death and dying.

Remember? Denial, anger, bargaining, depression, and finally, acceptance. The dying go through these stages and so do those standing by. The time of bereavement will probably produce them again and you may feel like your life is a rerun of some oft-seen TV program. Don't be impatient or discouraged, just remember the ultimate goal of these stages is to get to acceptance.

Karen was a gal who had worked her way through those stages to acceptance. Six months before she died, she said to one of our pastors, "Keith, whatever time I have left, I'm not going to leave sad, grief-stricken memories. But by the grace of God, I'm going to leave happy, victorious times and memories for my family." And so she *did!* But, like her family and those of us who are left behind, we must remember those difficult stages may appear many months after we think we are "over" our grief.

Just yesterday our eighteen-year-old daughter, Laurie, read my typed carbon copies of the first seven chapters of this book and wrote me a long letter. In part, it says:

My precious Mother,

I love you dearly, and after reading *Mourning Song*, I had to face the fact that someday I will have to say goodby to you . . . as you had to say goodby to your precious mother.

After reading the book I asked God to take you quickly when you are to "keep your appointment." But then, the more I thought about it, the more my mind changed . . . . You see, you learned so much from your mom and she left you with some of the most precious as well as valuable lessons *because* she died slowly. I want to learn all I can from you now, but I also want to gain a whole different area when you die. Not only do I feel this about you, but about Daddy, too.

To be honest, though, I don't want you to die at all. But because of your book, I think not only your death, but Dad's too—will be a *little* bit easier. Thank you for your book, Mom—I needed it!

Love,

LAURIE

Acceptance, standing on its shaky, newborn legs, has begun to live in Laurie's heart. In the years out ahead when death strikes at her parents, relatives, or friends she will have a giant head start in hearing the message and melody of acceptance.

A friend of mine stood by his father's casket and then wrote these brief lines. Out of his pen flowed his acceptance song:

> that which gave me life
> lies before me lifeless.
>
> the voice—the Golden Tenor—
> reposes—forever silent.
>
> but is it?
>
> perhaps in that Mysterious Realm
> a new voice is heard

to challenge the beauty of
celestial choirs.

perhaps
he who laughed so easily,
who loved life and
lived it with such gusto, and
who was at one equally with
peasants or kings
this very moment
has audience with
the King of Kings.

earth is poorer now—
yet richer
for having known him.

If the first part of God's restoration song begins with forgiveness, and then moves into the melody of acceptance, it is the incredible finale of hope that brings me up out of my seat to applaud and shout, "Bravo!"

3. *Hope.*

God gives hope in several ways, but one of the best is with the poetry He has written through others.

As I look back now, I can see that just before I experienced the deaths of my son, grandfather, and mother, God was tuning up his orchestra for the song of hope.

Only a bare two months before David died, a friend of mine introduced me to the writings of Martha Snell Nicholson. What seemed then like a casual remark by Al Sanders—"Joyce, you'll love her poems," turned out to be far more succinct than imagined.

I can see in retrospect that God deliberately turned my heart to her writings. What made her poems special was that she wrote all of them while confined to her bed as an invalid. She had been ill for twenty-five years with five major diseases (including cancer) and had lost her father and beloved husband. But her work was special for another reason. While it was not blissfully ignorant or saccharine-sweet like an anesthetic which blocks out anger, pain, or sorrow, it was honest (sometimes blunt) and realistically filled with God's hope.

During the dark months of blindly stumbling around, trying to heal physically from the surgery and emotionally from David's death, I received hundreds of letters which included poems. Most of them only made me angry. The only lights that shone were in this poem, "Broken Dreams," and I suppose the reason it really reached me was that *finally* someone admitted that my dream was broken. It said:

Broken Dreams

I do not hold my broken dreams
And cling to them and weep,
Beseeching God to mend them now.
I give them back to Him
From Whom they came, . . .
And a secret joy lightens all my days,
And long sweet nights I dream
Of how it fares with them in Heaven.

I fill my little day
With little tasks,
I give the best I have
To him who asks.
Years that are full
More quickly pass.

Some day the stars will shine again,
The flowers bloom,
And all the winds blow sweet.
Some day,
In Heaven's golden dawning,
Will tender angels give them back to me,
My broken dreams—unbroken then,
All loveliness,
Complete.

MARTHA SNELL NICHOLSON

Somehow, because of the hope of the last five lines, I held together. I filled my "little day with little tasks" and I tried—oh, how I tried!

Then, when my mother died, I received this letter from my millionaire friend, Mary Korstjens.

Dearest Joyce,

You and your family are on my mind and heart so much these days. The book of poems by Martha Snell Nicholson that you lent me once, had the two poems I have enclosed. They were very precious to me when my mom went to be with God.

Joyce, may God's love sustain and strengthen you beyond belief.

All my love and prayers,
MARY

One of those poems was called, "Along the Golden Streets," by Martha Snell Nicholson, and it was poignantly beautiful and rang the bells of comfort in my heart; but the other one became my theme song over the next years. I still never read it without thinking of the pain-racked, bedridden little lady who stubbornly refused to give in to her own agony and penned:

The Heart Held High

God made me a gift of laughter
And a heart held high,
Knowing what life would bring me
By and by,

Seeing my roses wither
One by one,
Hearing my life-song falter,
Scarce begun,

Watching me walk with Sorrow. . . .
That is why
He made me this gift of laughter—
This heart held high!

MARTHA SNELL NICHOLSON

Martha Snell Nicholson also helped me in my concept of what death is really all about by this poem:

The Other Side

This isn't death—it's glory!
It is not dark—it's light!

It isn't stumbling, groping,
Or even faith—it's sight!
This isn't grief—it's having
My last tear wiped away;
It's sunrise—it's the morning
Of my eternal day!

This isn't even praying—
It's speaking face to face;
Listening and glimpsing
The wonders of His grace.
This is the end of pleading
For strength to bear my pain;
Not even pain's dark mem'ry
Will ever live again.

How did I bear the earth-life
Before I came up higher,
Before my soul was granted
Its ev'ry deep desire,
Before I knew this rapture
Of meeting face to face
The One who sought me, saved me,
And kept me by His grace!

By her writings, I found Mrs. Nicholson did not live in denial, anger, bargaining, or depression, but in a hope-filled acceptance of life *and* dying. She was on honest terms with the agonies of pain and I loved her work the most when she wrote, after the death of her husband:

Teach Me to Walk Alone

I live now in a strange new land
Where I must walk alone,
Where I must smile without a tear,
And grief must make no moan.

My comfort and my guiding star,
My tower of strength, has gone.
No peace descends to me with dusk,
No light breaks with my dawn.

The habit of his loving heart
Was thoughtfulness for me.
And yet that heart has ceased to beat. . . .
Lord, how can such things be?

My arms have found if they reach out
They clasp but empty air;
And though I search the silent rooms
I never find him there.

I had to learn to walk, dear Lord,
When I was young and small.
Teach me again, for of myself
I can do naught at all!

Our hearts are mended by poetry, especially the honest, valid work borne out of heartaches and matured by God's direction.

Our souls are also healed by prose writings and songs.

God used Dr. Elisabeth Kübler-Ross's book as well as His Own Word, and eventually He led me to books (sometimes just a paragraph or two) which spoke directly and decisively to my needs.

The strongest writing, filled with the most hope, I found was God's Word.

To His friend, Martha, Jesus laid on the line our unconquerable position as Christians on hope and life after death when He said:

I am the one who raises the dead and gives them life again. Anyone who believes in me, even though he dies like anyone else, shall live again.
John 11:25

These powerful words transform "I *guess* so," and "I *hope* so," and "I *wish* so," into "I KNOW SO!"

The vigor and the vitality of Jesus' words fill in the missing parts in the musical arrangement of my mourning song. John picks up the refrain for me whenever I read his words:

And what is it that God has said? That he has given us eternal life, and that this life is in his Son. So whoever has God's Son has life; whoever does not have his Son, does not have life.
1 John 5:11, 12

So, if you are a Christian (one who has believed on the Lord
Jesus Christ; who has asked for forgiveness of sins) then you have
been *guaranteed* life—not just here, but forever. This hope sepa-
rates the men from the boys, the women from the girls; so we, who
have Christ, can look death, dying, and sorrow right on, eyeball-to-
eyeball, and not flinch. Death is ugly and it is repulsive, but it is
not, I repeat, *not* able to bring the life of a Christian to a dreadful,
screeching halt. God has worked out an alternate plan and it is a
plan filled with soaring hope.

When Bernie D. Zondervan died, his publishing house printed
many of the letters which were received from Christians all over the
world. It was an inspiring booklet to read. I've selected only two
of the comments, but because of the hope they contain, I think
you should read them.

I know you [Pat Zondervan—Bernie's brother] see the blessings in the
experience. You have told us often of Bernie's faith. You share with us
the Christian convictions concerning the joy and gain which now are his.
But nevertheless death for the moment is disruptive. Earthly ties are
precious and they don't break easily. Moreover, I think you two brothers
were unusually close. But the thing which made you close was your
mutual service of the Lord. That goes on. Bernie's in heaven and yours
on this earth. And one day you will be reunited in glory. I like John 14:3.
I think it is Christ's description of the death of a Christian. "I will come
again." The Lord took Bernie. Not cancer, not weakness. Nothing but the
Lord. That is most comforting. "And receive you unto myself." That's
what's happened to him. He's with the Lord. All of us here below live by
faith. But faith at best is weak. It varies. One day it's rich and strong.
The next it's weak and feeble. But Bernie lives now by sight. He's with
the Lord. That is far better. We sorrow, but not as the world.

REV. JOHN A. DE KRUYTER, PASTOR
Seymour Christian Reformed Church

There was a time when I would have expressed my regrets in the learning of Bernie's passing, but that was before I fully understood what he
passed INTO . . . and not for the world would I ever wish his presence
here, when he has so much of great joy in sharing there—His is by far
the better place than that which you and I share today. In some respects,
I am sure that I become a bit anxious for the appointed day myself—I
hope that you and I can join in a jubilation meeting there soon, together.

HEARTSILL WILSON
America's Dynamic Voice of Marketing

In the beautiful book *Home Before Dark,* by Bryant M. Kirkland, three sentences stand out vividly:

The hope of heaven fills a need in modern man in answer to his profound search for meaning in existence.

In an age that says there is no meaning, human nature paradoxically cries out for even more meaning.

Without the hope of heaven human existence loses much of its nerve and significance.

It is this hope of heaven, this shining promise of life after death, that restores our confidence. The lovely confidence I saw in my mother while she was dying began to grow in my heart after she died, once I realized what a wealth of restoration was in the Christian's hope.

An army chaplain, a real man of God, Colonel Jack Randles, lent me an old book of his. It was called *God's Trombones* and it was a beautiful collection of sermons by a very forceful, creative black preacher. The chaplain knew as I read the book I'd get to the sermon on death and he felt it would give me a brand-new conception of dying and bring its own unique restoration. He was so right.

If you can, read it out loud, as I have done many, many times; and you will find it will reach out from the printed page and touch you with its intrinsic honesty.

With each line, I can breathe a sigh of thanks to God. "Someone has cried like I, someone else has hurt, someone else has tried to fathom the depths of sorrowing and they have succeeded in articulating it on paper so well—I can understand it better now."

Go Down Death

> Weep not, weep not
> She is not dead;
> She's resting in the bosom of Jesus.
> Heart-broken husband—weep no more;
> Grief-stricken son—weep no more;
> Left-lonesome daughter—weep no more;
> She's only just gone home.

Day before yesterday morning,
God was looking down from his great, high heaven,
Looking down on all his children,
And his eye fell on Sister Caroline,
Tossing on her bed of pain.
And God's big heart was touched with pity,
With the everlasting pity.

And God sat back on his throne,
And he commanded that tall, bright angel standing at
    his right hand:
Call me Death!
And that tall, bright angel cried in a voice
That broke like a clap of thunder:
Call Death!—Call Death!
And the echo sounded down the streets of heaven
Till it reached away back to that shadowy place,
Where Death waits with his pale, white horses.

And Death heard the summons,
And he leaped on his fastest horse,
Pale as a sheet in the moonlight.
Up the golden street Death galloped,
And the hoofs of his horse struck fire from the gold,
But they didn't make no sound.
Up Death rode to the Great White Throne,
And waited for God's command.

And God said: Go down, Death, go down,
Go down to Savannah, Georgia,
Down in Yamacraw,
And find Sister Caroline.
She's borne the burden and heat of the day,
She's labored long in my vineyard,
And she's tired—
She's weary—
Go down, Death, and bring her to me.

And Death didn't say a word,
But he loosed the reins on his pale, white horse,
And he clamped the spurs to his bloodless sides,
And out and down he rode,
Through heaven's pearly gates,

Past suns and moons and stars;
On Death rode,
And the foam from his horse was like a comet in the sky;
On Death rode,
Leaving the lightning's flash behind;
Straight on down he came.

While we were watching round her bed,
She turned her eyes and looked away,
She saw what we couldn't see;
She saw Old Death. She saw Old Death
Coming like a falling star.
But Death didn't frighten Sister Caroline;
He looked to her like a welcome friend.
And she whispered to us: I'm going home,
And she smiled and closed her eyes.

And Death took her up like a baby,
And she lay in his icy arms,
But she didn't feel no chill.
And Death began to ride again—
Up beyond the evening star,
Out beyond the morning star,
Into the glittering light of glory,
Onto the Great White Throne.
And there he laid Sister Caroline
On the loving breast of Jesus.

And Jesus took his own hand and wiped away her tears,
And he smoothed the furrows from her face,
And the angels sang a little song,
And Jesus rocked her in his arms,
And kept a-saying: Take your rest,
Take your rest, take your rest.

Weep not—weep not,
She is not dead;
She's resting in the bosom of Jesus.

JAMES WELDON JOHNSON

I'm not sure how many times God has used the message of "Go Down Death" in my life, but He certainly has healed and restored my spirit as He promised me He'd do in the Twenty-Third Psalm.

Ever since the world began we have been experiencing life and death. The dying part of living has been with us in the past and it will remain with us in the future until God Himself calls an end to this existence as we know it.

My soul can accept the realities of death and dying, the sorrows of grieving, and the living I must continue to do, if I am willing to listen to God's song.

The early Christians heard the mourning song of God and as they were being led to their horrendous deaths in the Roman arena, they picked up mourning song's tune and we are told "went to their death—*singing*." It is not possible to be scared to death and still sing. The vocal cords restrict themselves into hard, rigid, tautly pulled ropes that will not work. So those martyred Christians had to have the song of God's confidence and joy really bursting within them in order to have filled the Coliseum with the sound of their music.

When I read, "Tears of joy shall stream down their faces, and I will lead them home with great care" (Jeremiah 31:9), I can, in my mind's eye, see not only those early Christians, but all the precious children of God we have lost; and, as if they are being filmed for a great movie spectacular, they stand together, all on a supersized screen. They stand as a gigantic host of people in front of me and the stereophonic music pours out of hundreds of speakers over my soul. Beautifully, as I listen and watch, I see God leading them *home*—with "great care."

Over the visual picture and above the sound of the triumphant music, I hear the narrator. He reads from a script written by Jeremiah and his reasonant words ring deep and clear:

They shall come home and sing songs of joy upon the hills of Zion, and shall be radiant over the goodness of the Lord. . . . Their life shall be like a watered garden, and all their sorrows shall be gone.

Jeremiah 31:12

They are not the only ones who can sing the songs of Zion—we who are left can sing, too. We are not suffering from frozen vocal cords that are stiff because of fear, absent because of denial, or tight because of anger and bitterness that would give us laryngitis.

Forgiveness, acceptance, and hope have warmed and toned up the flexibility of the vocal cords; and so with full, strong, healthy voices we can sing the songs of restoration and hope!

We can sing the old hymns of the church like Fanny Crosby's "Blessed Assurance," or Spafford's and Bliss's "It Is Well With My Soul," or the song J. A. Crutchfield wrote called "Zion's Hill," with the very boldness and confidence of God.

We can sing the newer songs of restoration like Bill Gaither's "He Touched Me," Audrey Mieir's "Don't Spare Me," or Ruth Calkin's "But I Do Know" with God's authority giving a positive, honest reality to our vocal tones.

And we can sing songs like this one:

He Giveth More

He giveth more grace when the burdens grow greater,
He sendeth more strength when the labors increase;
To added affliction He addeth His mercy,
To multiplied trials, His multiplied peace.

When we have exhausted our store of endurance,
When our strength has failed ere the day is half done,
When we reach the end of our hoarded resources,
Our Father's full giving is only begun.

His love has no limit, His grace has no measure,
His power no boundary known unto men;
For out of His infinite riches in Jesus
He giveth and giveth and giveth again.

ANNIE JOHNSON FLINT

We can sing because we *know* Hope and we *experience* Hope daily! Because of Hope's song, we can move, work, and make our time here really count.

My mother wanted me to hear the song of hope, to be restored by it after she was gone, and then act on it. She wrote:

God bless your ministry, my dear Joyce, I pray your work for Him will be blessed far and wide.

The world needs our *testimony* in *whatever* way we are gifted to give it!

Let's be true and press toward God's mark (His plan and purpose for our lives) of the *High Calling!*

Remember, we have Him and by His life *we* have life!

So I have listened and heard this remarkable song. The hope of the music creeps over the hills and valleys of my life and heals, warms, and motivates me to action. I *can* carry on, I *can* last, I can even *sing* because of the aliveness of God in my soul.

The sound of God's powerful lasting song of restoration has begun with the opening theme of forgiveness; and finally it arrives at the chorus and final *coda* with hope, glorious hope, *crescendo*ing up around us in fully orchestrated, stereophonic sound!

It is as we *allow* our ears to hear this concluding section of music that God reveals the full-blown beauty of His tender, moving, mourning song.

It is also this part, the hope part of the song, which lingers in our minds. Long after the song has ended, even during those dark, forbidding hours just before dawn, we can recall the lyric and melody line of hope; and to our amazement we can sing the heady, glorious song for whatever life-span we have left!